FAITH FORWARD FUTURE

FAITH FORWARD FUTURE

Moving Past Your Disappointments,
Delays, and Destructive Thinking

CHAD VEACH

NELSON
BOOKS

An Imprint of Thomas Nelson

Published in Nashville, Tennessee, by Nelson Books, an imprint of Thomas Nelson. Nelson Books and Thomas Nelson are registered trademarks of HarperCollins Christian Publishing, Inc.

Published in association with the literary agency of The FEDD Agency, Inc., P.O. Box 341973, Austin, Texas, 78734.

Thomas Nelson titles may be purchased in bulk for educational, business, fundraising, or sales promotional use. For information, please e-mail SpecialMarkets@ThomasNelson.com.

Any Internet addresses, phone numbers, or company or product information printed in this book are offered as a resource and are not intended in any way to be or to imply an endorsement by Thomas Nelson, nor does Thomas Nelson vouch for the existence, content, or services of these sites, phone numbers, companies, or products beyond the life of this book.

Unless otherwise noted, Scripture quotations are taken from the Holy Bible, New International Version®, NIV®. Copyright © 1973, 1978, 1984, 2011 by Biblica, Inc.® Used by permission of Zondervan. All rights reserved worldwide. www.zondervan.com. The "NIV" and "New International Version" are trademarks registered in the United States Patent and Trademark Office by Biblica, Inc.®

Scripture quotations marked NKJV are taken from the New King James Version®. © 1982 by Thomas Nelson. Used by permission. All rights reserved.

Scripture quotations marked THE MESSAGE are taken from The Message. Copyright © by Eugene H. Peterson 1993, 1994, 1995, 1996, 2000, 2001, 2002. Used by permission of Tyndale House Publishers, Inc.

Scripture quotations marked ESV are taken from the ESV® Bible (The Holy Bible, English Standard Version®). Copyright © 2001 by Crossway, a publishing ministry of Good News Publishers. Used by permission. All rights reserved.

Scripture quotations marked HCSB are taken from the Holman Christian Standard Bible®. Copyright © 1999, 2000, 2002, 2003, 2009 by Holman Bible Publishers. Used by permission. HCSB® is a federally registered trademark of Holman Bible Publishers.

ISBN 978-0-7180-3839-7 (eBook)

Library of Congress Cataloging-in-Publication Data
Names: Veach, Chad, 1979- author.
Title: Faith forward future : moving past disappointments, delays, and destructive thinking / Chad Veach.
Description: Nashville : Thomas Nelson, [2017] | Includes bibliographical references.
Identifiers: LCCN 2017008574 | ISBN 9780718038373
Subjects: LCSH: Dreams--Religious aspects--Christianity.
Classification: LCC BR115.D74 V43 2017 | DDC 248.4--dc23 LC record available at https://lccn.loc.gov/2017008574

Printed in the United States of America
18 19 20 21 LSC 6 5 4

to julia.
you live this book every day
you are my true hero
i love you

CONTENTS

Part One
THE DREAM
What should we be chasing?

Chapter One

WHEN LIFE DOESN'T WORK OUT

My phone was screaming at me from the middle console of my car, shouting that it was time to pull the trigger and make "the call."

It was the reason I had driven out to the middle of nowhere. I had escaped the noise of friends, family, and my world. I had committed that I would finally do the thing I had been avoiding doing for months.

I would end the relationship with the girl I should've broken up with a long time ago.

It wasn't because she was a bad person or that she was ruining my life, but, quite simply, it was a relationship I knew I wasn't supposed to be in. From the very start, it had felt like I was pushing against the world and even God himself to make things work. I was ignoring the signs that popped up at every turn. My work was hurting, my vitality was zapped, my friendships were crumbling around me, and a booming voice was telling me to stop before things got worse.

The phone screamed at me again.

Even though it was silently sitting there. No phone calls coming in. No one waiting for me on the other line.

But I couldn't reach for it yet and dial those numbers. Because to end things meant to end my dream. It would mean the death of a future me, standing in a suit, looking on as she walked down the aisle in a white dress. The death of the future I had been set on from day one—the romance and the life I had drawn up for myself. I know what you're thinking. *But you're married to Julia Veach! How could life get any better than that?* Don't worry, people. I'm beyond grateful God's better plan prevailed in the end, but in that moment, I couldn't see it. And even the idea of letting go of this dream I *could* see felt incredibly painful.

It was this original, flawed dream that had helped me drown out those resounding alarm bells all along the way. I had been clinging to it like a toddler clings to a toy he's been told not to play with. When God clearly communicated his no, I either ignored him or tried to convince myself that he was telling me something else.

SOMETIMES YOU HAVE TO LAY TO REST YOUR DREAM TO GIVE LIFE TO GOD'S DREAM.

The phone shouted at me again.

This time, instead of recalling the dream, I recalled the nightmare. The nightmare my disobedience had led me to: the crumbling ministry, the disappointed family, the rejected friends. The plan I had laid out for myself had failed miserably.

So I finally picked up the phone and made the call. I listened to confused crying on the other end and tried to hide my own similar emotions. With one conversation, I broke two hearts.

That day I began to learn that sometimes you have to lay to rest your dream to give life to God's dream.

BROKEN DREAMS

I live in Los Angeles, a place that many have named the "City of Broken Dreams." Each year thousands of people move here, hoping to make it as a director, actor, musician, or reality TV star. Because the industry is highly competitive and there's only room for so many to be the next big thing, many fail at achieving their dreams.

With an estimated 254,000 men, women, and children sleeping on the streets each night and also twenty of the world's small number of billionaires in residence here, the city is a paradox. It's a picture of how society views both success and failure, achievement and heartbreak, arriving and losing. But this city is only a microcosm of the state of the world.

In a *Social Forces* study, researchers found that only 6 percent of people end up in the career they dreamed of as a child.[1] Obviously, many conditions can cause you to veer from the path to becoming the firefighter or astronaut or ballerina you once thought you'd be, but this dismal number proves that many people's lives don't go the way they planned. Though often this is a good thing (thank God I didn't pursue that DJ career), our broken dreams can leave us feeling disappointed and affect the way we view our worth and potential.

The reality is that we don't always accomplish all that we set out to do. Our lives don't always turn out the way we hoped they would. We dream of a relationship with a certain person, a career path, or a perfect family. And when those dreams don't work out, like my own relationship didn't, we're left to wonder . . .

Where do I go from here?

What do I dream of now?

Should I throw in the towel?

Because God gives us free will, we get to experience what it looks like to mess up and destroy our lives. And mess up our lives we often do.

While working as a youth pastor and dating long-distance, I refused to listen to the advice of others and even the voice of God about ending my relationship. I had my dream, and I was set on making it happen. Because of this, I was ignoring people I should have been more focused on, the youth ministry I was running was shrinking, and I started failing at what God had called me to do. I could barely look people in the eye.

Eventually, I came out on the other side of the heartbreak with an understanding of God's better plan. But my decisions delayed my destiny, and it took a while to truly move past the pain of the whole experience.

THE PRODIGAL DREAM

My story, like yours, is beautifully depicted in Jesus' parable about the prodigal son in Luke 15. It's the story of a father with a son who asked for his inheritance early. Though the father knew the request was a bad idea, he granted it, and, in return, the boy took the money and squandered it.

With his free will, the son pursued his dream. He chased after what Jesus described as "wild living" (v. 13). And, ultimately, he failed.

He failed hard.

The father in the story knew his son was headed for disaster.

You want to test the waters out there? he probably thought. *You want to go mess up your life? That's fine. I would love to protect you from all of that, but you made your choice.*

Jesus said that, once the son's money ran out, "he went and hired himself out to a citizen of that country, who sent him to his fields to feed pigs." He went from living the dream to living in the pen with pigs and even "long[ing] to fill his stomach with the pods that the pigs were eating" (vv. 15–16).

It's while the son was filled with disappointment and coping with his failure that the story takes a turn. Jesus told us that when the son was in the pen he started to remember his father's house. He started to recall his father's servants and how even they had food to eat and a bed to sleep in. "So he got up and went to his father" (v. 20).

In his darkest moment, he remembered that things were better his father's way. He didn't know if his father would accept him back as a son, but he did leave that pen with a confidence that whatever his father had for him, it would be better than his current situation.

The story ends with the father, a picture of God and his perfect love for us, running to his son, throwing his arms around him, bringing him back into the family, and honoring him with a huge party. It's what Kanye West and I like to call the "God Dream."

> **YOUR MOST RECENT FAILURE IS ONLY A MINOR SETBACK FOR A MAJOR COMEBACK.**

And it's what God, your Father, is waiting to give you. Despite your brokenness, despite the failure of your own plan, God is still ready to take you into his future.

When you find yourself in the pen, or

in the car making the phone call, remember how God views your broken dream. He looks at you and says, "Your most recent failure is only a minor setback for a major comeback."

Success often looks different from the way the world paints it. God's plan is so much more than career gain or financial security. When we fail to hit the targets we've set, we often beat ourselves up or fail to see the better future God has in store.

It took me an embarrassingly long time to finally make that phone call, but once I did, I started to realize the major comeback God had in mind for me. It was less than a year later that I went to celebrate Thanksgiving with my family as a single man who was starting to rebuild his life after his big blunder. At that dinner, I was reintroduced to a childhood friend who soon became my girlfriend and ultimately became my wife. She was definitely a God Dream.

In the end, the father's plan was better for his son, and God's plan was far better for me. I'm convinced it's better for you too.

Chapter Two
CALLING OUT GREATNESS

We all have that friend who always seems to be talking up something. I call this person "the hype man," and there's one in every group. You're probably thinking of yours right now. If you have a hard time pinpointing one, you probably *are* that person. Maybe you're the one constantly hyping a new restaurant, or a new band, or a hip coffee shop you recently tried. The hype man typically gets excited about anything new, and nothing is off-limits. I find it especially entertaining when hype men talk up new people they've only recently met, as if these new acquaintances were the next big thing.

"Oh my gosh! You have to meet Rick. Rick is so funny. You will die laughing when you meet him. He's, like, the funniest person I've ever met. Ever."

If you are not the hype man but you have a hype-man friend, you know the drill. Due to experience, you've probably created a little equation in your mind: whatever the hype man says, you always have to cut it in half.

"This new TV show will change your life!" You listen politely and then prepare to have your life only marginally changed, if at all. You calculate that the reality is you'll only mildly enjoy maybe an episode or two.

"Every song on the new album will make you cry!" You decide to prepare for a small emotional effect. You don't even bother grabbing a tissue before you listen to it. You know that you will likely discover the truth like you always have before, and your expectations will be crushed again.

The reality always seems to be that the TV show was all right, the album was forgettable, and Rick? Rick isn't actually that funny. Yes, maybe he sent a funny meme in a group text one time, but that doesn't make him a stand-up comedian. We can all send funny memes. It's not that impressive, Rick.

The other day my wife, Julia, was hyping up a restaurant to me. And this restaurant wasn't just any restaurant. Its specialty was Mediterranean food. And Mediterranean food isn't just any food. It's my absolute favorite. Give me some pita bread and some hummus, and I'll start a revival.

Julia knows this about me, and that I have extremely strong attachments to my favorite Mediterranean places, and yet she still sold this place to me as "the bessssssstttt Mediterranean food you will everrrrr eat!"

I would die when I tried it.

It would blow my mind.

I would never be the same again.

Her hype-man game was strong. And so, naturally, I nodded my head and said, "I can't wait, babe." But inside, I pulled out the ol' Hype Calculator and cut her assessment of this restaurant's deliciousness in half.

Later that day she went to the supposedly mind-blowing place and brought some food back to the house. This is because when I eat Mediterranean food, I like to do it in the privacy of my own home so I can savagely devour my pita bread and hummus with no strangers staring at me. I don't need you to watch me crush those kebabs, okay?

To my surprise, the food was as good as she had described it. I demolished it! My mind was indeed blown! My expectations were exceeded! I would truly never be the same again!

It's easy to be skeptical of hype. We don't want to believe the unbelievable, because our past experiences have proven that it's just that: unbelievable. So when someone tells us that we could have access to an even better life than the one we have imagined for ourselves, that we have the potential to walk out in amazing purpose, and that our future could be "above and beyond all that we ask or think" (Ephesians 3:20 HCSB), it's natural to cut statements like these in half in our brains—even when they come from the Word of God.

Something inside of all of us hears these words and says, "Don't go playing with my heart." We remember the things we've tried and failed to accomplish in our lives. We recall the disappointment and say, "Never again." We fear that we could be part of some spiritual prank. Maybe God is just setting up some elaborate *PUNK'd* episode where we're the butt of the joke.

Does God really have something more for me? What if this promise of "above and beyond" isn't actually my destiny, and I find myself cruelly disappointed again? we wonder.

Because we live in a cynical world, where a hype man's words are met with eye rolls and mistrust, it's hard for us to

WHERE CYNICISM SAYS, "YOU CAN'T," GOD SAYS, "WITH ME, YOU CAN."

imagine the possibilities and all that God has in store. But where cynicism says, "You can't," God says, "With me, you can."

HE DELIVERS

Let's talk about someone who encountered a person who delivered on all the hype. At the start of his story, this someone really had no idea what was possible for an average guy like him. I like to imagine that he, like most of us, started off life with a dream, some image of what his tomorrow might look like. But, in the end, God led him somewhere that exceeded all the expectations this man had for his future. When God came along, it didn't matter if he had achieved everything he set out to do, because there was something better in store for him.

His name was Simon.

You'll find him in the Bible, and he was a good little Jewish boy who always did as he was told, honored the Sabbath, didn't touch bacon, and fished for a living. This was his lot in life. I'm sure his dream looked a little something like this: fish, maybe start a family, have some kids, and then more fishing.

But then in walked possibility.

The story takes place in John 1, but before we ever see Simon and his encounter with this possibility, we meet a man named John, who sets the stage. Most people know him as "John the Baptist." Not because he was a fiery preacher from the South, but because he liked to baptize people in Jesus' name. He was baptizing people before Jesus even walked onto the scene. God gave him the job of preparing the way for Jesus' ministry.

In John 1:35–36, we see him doing just that. The passage says, "The next day John was there again with two of his disciples. When he saw Jesus passing by, he said, 'Look, the Lamb of God!'"

John was so over-the-moon excited to meet Jesus that he shouted out to him. This enthusiasm was obviously contagious, because the story continues this way:

> When the two disciples heard him say this, they followed Jesus. Turning around, Jesus saw them following and asked, "What do you want?"
>
> They said, "Rabbi" (which means "Teacher"), "where are you staying?"
>
> "Come," he replied, "and you will see."
>
> So they went and saw where he was staying, and they spent that day with him. (vv. 37–39)

Incidentally, Andrew, Simon's brother, was one of these two disciples, and after he spent the day with Jesus, he rushed to tell his brother and brought him to meet this Lamb of God.

At last, we've arrived at Simon's big moment—the moment when, despite his own goals or the dreams he may have failed at achieving, possibility opens up for him. This was the start of his journey with Jesus. The story continues with Jesus looking at Simon and saying, "You are Simon son of John. You will be called Cephas" (v. 42).

In their very first encounter, Jesus started speaking destiny and future over him. To understand what Jesus was laying out, let's examine this word *Cephas*. It's Aramaic, meaning "rock," also translated "Peter" in Greek. Why was this significant? Much later in the story, after Simon declared Jesus as the long-awaited Savior of the world, Jesus used this word again. He pronounced,

"And I tell you that you are Peter, and on this rock I will build my church, and the gates of Hades will not overcome it" (Matthew 16:18).

God already knew what he had in store for Simon. Even though this initial encounter recorded in John 1 was just the beginning of their relationship, Jesus knew the end of the story. Because he is the Alpha and the Omega, the beginning and the end, he wanted to begin the process of revealing his plan for Peter's life right from the start. Though Jesus didn't explain it to him fully at that moment—and I'm sure Simon was a bit confused—Jesus knew what Simon's tomorrow held.

> **AM I TOO DISTRACTED BY THE SOUNDS OF FAILURE TO HEAR THE BEAUTIFUL FUTURE GOD IS SPEAKING OVER ME?**

And he knows what your tomorrow holds too. If you learn to listen, you may discover he has a name change specifically for you. How amazing would that be? But to hear it, you have to first be listening. Ask yourself, "Am I too distracted by the sounds of failure to hear the beautiful future God is speaking over me?"

If we move forward to Simon's next encounter with Jesus, we again see Jesus speak a huge future over his life. In Luke 5 and Matthew 4, the fisherman still didn't know much about Jesus' background or pedigree when he encountered him on the Lake of Gennesaret. These gospels tell us that this encounter occurred on a day when Peter had caught no fish. It was in this moment of complete failure and inability to do his job that God stepped in and revealed the plan.

Jesus was preaching to a large crowd nearby and used Simon's boat as a platform. Once his sermon was finished, he asked Simon to throw his net into the water again. Simon replied to Jesus' request this way: "Master, we've worked hard all night and haven't caught anything. But because you say so, I will let down the nets" (Luke 5:5).

At this point in Simon's story, he still had no clue that Jesus was the fulfillment of all the prophecies he had grown up hearing and studying. But Simon did as Jesus told him to do and threw his net into the water. Instantly, he witnessed a miracle as his net filled with fish. At that moment, I'm sure he saw another glimpse of the possibility that comes with Jesus. So when Jesus followed this miraculous act with a statement, Simon knew Jesus would deliver on whatever he promised. He knew Jesus' next words were worth pursuing, even though they did sound weird and seemingly impossible.

And Jesus' statement *was* a little weird. In Luke 5:10, he again laid out his plan for "the Rock." He showed Simon a glimpse of the better dream he had in store for him. Jesus came to him in his moment of disappointment and frustration with failing and told Simon what he could accomplish with him. The verse says, "Then Jesus said to Simon, 'Don't be afraid; from now on you will fish for people.'"

If I were Simon, I might have a hard time following the "don't be afraid" order, even after witnessing a miracle. And "fish for people"? What does that even mean? Is there bait and a fishing pole involved?

But despite the strange message, something inside of Simon trusted the words of Jesus. Simon knew that Jesus would ultimately show him how this "fishing for people" thing would work. He knew he'd deliver on this promise, as well as the promise that Simon would one day live up to the name Cephas.

WHO WOULD'VE THOUGHT?

When I was twenty-one years old and fresh out of Bible college, I worked at a church in Los Angeles. The church had a huge youth ministry, and, initially, I was excited to be a part of it. This was the life I had always dreamed of. It seemed I had truly accomplished what I had set out to do.

But if you've ever set out to accomplish a goal or life plan, you know that things don't always go as perfectly as you imagine. And in my case, the situation turned ugly.

Money issues. Drama in leadership. Crazy, stressful things were happening left and right. And suddenly I was standing in the middle of my dream, watching it crumble around me. I remember sitting in my office, asking God, "Why do you have me here?"

I was ready to prepare an escape plan and get as far from that church as I could. *That's it. I give up. This so-called dream isn't worth the daily stress and emotional turmoil.* I'm not proud of how I wanted to flee when my perfect job turned out to be a lie, but that was the reality.

In my prayer, I expected God to give me a way out. I expected a sign from the future. I banked on him turning my empty boat into one overflowing with fish. But God surprised me. And not in a good way—at least in my estimation at the time.

Instead of encouraging me to leave, he asked me to stay. Just like Simon was probably confused by Jesus' strange "fishers of people" line, I had a hard time wrapping my mind around why God would want me to remain in such a toxic situation. It didn't make any sense, but I felt it was the right thing to do. I felt like he was telling me that I needed to learn everything I could from the church—flaws and all.

I've learned over the years that sometimes you come to God for a nice, safe answer, and instead he gives you a challenge that seems anything but. Ultimately, I made a decision like Simon's. I decided that, despite God's confusing direction, I would stick around and see what was possible, because I knew he was capable of the miraculous.

Let's fast-forward to two years later. I found myself on New Year's Day 2004, waking up with a strange feeling. Something big was about to happen. Do you ever have one of those days where you walk around with a knot in your stomach, knowing that at any moment a good thing is about to go down and that good thing might change everything for the better? It was one of *those* days.

And things did change. I received a phone call from a pastor in Seattle, my old stomping grounds. He was a leader I had come to know through our church circle, and he was asking me to come up and be the youth pastor at his church in Puyallup, Washington.

I told my current boss and my pastors immediately; I knew it was time. It was for this opportunity that God had asked me to stick around.

This happened only days after January 1, but by March 4, I was up in Puyallup. I was full of passion and excitement because I was right where God wanted me to be! I had waited just like he told me to, and he had provided this awesome opportunity! Things were going to play out perfectly, right?

Wrong. The first youth meeting I held, a measly fifty kids showed up. My dreams were shattered again.

I know I should've been excited, but I had just left a thriving youth ministry in LA with hundreds of teenagers. And there I was, standing in front of only fifty. They all stared blankly back at me.

"God, what did I do wrong? Did I hear you incorrectly? Am I supposed to be here?" I asked.

Again, I felt God tell me, "Just trust me."

"Just watch."

"See what happens here."

As he did with Simon, he was leading me to do things I didn't quite understand. But also like Simon, I was game for the ride. Jesus showed Simon a glimpse of possibility when he filled his nets with fish, and he was doing the same with me. In that moment after the first night of youth group, God placed an image in my head.

I had created a vision that represented my definition of success, which was that I'd run a youth ministry with maybe a couple of hundred kids, making an impact on the few. But God had something way bigger in mind. He showed me a vision of thousands of students. He showed me lives changing for the better and a whole city being impacted. He showed me the picture of possibility.

I wouldn't stand in that picture for five years. And during the five years leading up to it, things weren't always easy. I definitely wasn't always perfect. I made mistakes. I failed countless times. But God had a plan during it all. He knew what was coming around the next corner. He knew who I would meet. He knew who he wanted me to become. He knew my potential and that my today looked different from my tomorrow.

Let's fast-forward even farther to the present. Since that day, God has been good to me in so many ways. Though I still fail and find myself delaying the things he has for me because of my own human weakness, and I still beat myself up over mistakes or failures, God keeps finding ways to lead me into his picture of success.

Who would've thought I'd meet my wife during all of this or that I would have the family I have today? Who would've thought that on the other side of a crazy-sounding decision to stay in a toxic situation for just a while longer, God would have something great for me?

IF YOU AREN'T WILLING TO DO RIDICULOUS THINGS, YOU'LL NEVER EXPERIENCE MIRACULOUS THINGS.

God would've thought, of course. I've learned over the years that if you aren't willing to do ridiculous things, you'll never experience miraculous things.

FOUR MINUTES

A friend once told me a story about an awkward encounter he'd had at a little kid's birthday party. Kids were playing all around a pool, adults were barbecuing and chatting, and he was standing there enjoying himself when a big dude walked up to him.

"How long can you hold your breath under water?" the guy asked out of nowhere. My friend had never met this man before, and this was his conversation opener.

"Uh, a minute probably. I don't know," he told the complete stranger.

"A minute?" the guy replied, almost angry at the answer. "I think you could do it for longer. Let's jump in the pool. Show me what you got."

I don't know if it was because this dude was quite large and towering over him or because he was so awkwardly demanding, but my friend agreed and jumped into the pool with this man he'd never met for an epic breath-holding challenge.

He plunged his head under the water and gave it all he had. When he popped up out of the water, the guy was there looking at the timer. It was one minute exactly! He did it! He reached his goal!

But the stranger wasn't impressed. "Actually, you know what?" he said. "I think you could do four minutes."

Four minutes? My friend was shocked. He had just given this challenge everything he had, and at a little kid's birthday party, no less!

"I don't think that's possible," he replied.

"Nope," the man snapped back. "You can do four minutes."

He was not going to take no for an answer. He started to talk about how it was all psychological, how we don't think we can hold our breath for longer than a minute but we physically can. He taught my friend how to think about things differently and showed him a technique that made this possible.

By the end of the party, my friend could hold his breath for four entire minutes. I'm not sure the birthday boy was too thrilled to have someone steal the limelight on his big day, but my friend left feeling pretty proud of his accomplishment and new skill.

So many of us are like my friend at this party. We can't see the God-given potential in ourselves. Oftentimes this is because we've failed in the past, and we're currently living with a broken dream. Sometimes it's because outside forces, like a broken family or a negative environment, have left us with a limited view of our worth. When someone walks up to us and sees our potential like Jesus did with Peter, it's usually hard for us to accept or believe. It's much easier to limit ourselves and only see the worst.

But God is like that stranger at the birthday party who instantly saw my friend's potential, only God sees even more. He sees your future and all you are capable of. He calls you "Rock." He says he's going to use you to build and grow something. He shows you a picture of a city changed for the better. You might view yourself as only being able to achieve a certain level of

> **REALIZING GOD'S PLAN FULLY IS UNDERSTANDING YOUR FULL POTENTIAL.**

success in this life, but God has something above and beyond in mind. And he'll stay committed until you walk in this potential. This is because realizing God's plan fully is understanding your full potential.

FROM SIMON TO THE ROCK

The most amazing part of Simon's story is that it doesn't end with the greatest fishing day of his life or with Jesus changing his name. It also doesn't end with a bunch of inspirational quotes from Jesus. Jesus doesn't just tell Simon, "This great thing will happen for you!" and then not deliver on such a promise. He isn't a fortune cookie or some meme on Instagram (thanks again, Rick).

The new name that Jesus gave him wasn't just for kicks; it came with an amazing new future. Because of Jesus, Simon transformed into a completely different person. Because of Jesus, he discovered what it really means to "live the dream."

Can I tell you how things ended for Peter? In John 1, Peter

was just a simple fisherman when he met Jesus for the first time, but soon he preached the first sermon in the history of the church. At the end of Acts 2, he proclaimed the truth about Jesus and saw three thousand people get saved. He also was the first person in the Upper Room on the day of Pentecost when the Holy Spirit came, and ultimately he helped spread the promise of the Holy Spirit to the Gentiles as well as the Jews. And it was Peter who went on to write books of the Bible and be powerfully used to build the church just like Jesus had promised.

> **REST IN THE REALITY THAT GOD HAS ALWAYS KNOWN YOU, ALWAYS CARED, AND ALWAYS SEEN YOUR FULL POTENTIAL.**

Simon Peter ultimately fulfilled all that God had intended for his life. He went from a man with a limited view of his future and who was a failure on the job to a man walking in his best possible tomorrow. And it all started with a simple thought: *Maybe there really is a God who has a plan for me. Maybe this God has something better than anything I could conjure up on my own.*

The life of Peter is proof that God has a plan, a crazy good plan. Rest in the reality that God has always known you, always cared, and always seen your full potential.

THE BEST IS YET TO COME

I don't think most people can fathom the greatness of their tomorrows. A lot of people don't see a picture in their heads of themselves affecting many lives. Many don't see a boat overflowing with fish, promises of a lifetime of possibility, or a name change that comes with a life change. This may be because that career they thought they'd have when they grew up didn't pan out, or the miracles they thought they'd be seeing in their marriage didn't happen.

Many of us have dead dreams. It's time to jumpstart and dream again. This time around, let's dream with God. His possibility is available to all. It's possibility like this that caused Peter to jump out of the boat and follow Jesus.

Peter's life is proof that God has a plan. It demonstrates that even if you're experiencing God for the first time, God has known you all along and has great things in store for you. Understanding the future that comes with God could be the game changer for your life. If you can see a glimpse of what God has in store for you, you might make a decision like Peter's to get out of the boat and follow him.

Think about your own life. What could God have for you? Will you write that book? Will you start that nonprofit? Will you influence art and culture? Will you change the world? What story is God waiting to write for you?

You might start thinking of your life and instantly feel unqualified. Because of failures, flaws, or missteps, you might feel you'll never accomplish anything truly remarkable. Later in the book, we'll explore how Peter is the prime example of someone who didn't always get it right. We'll also look at the lives of Paul, Jonah, David, Samson, and other heroes of the faith who made mistake after mistake. But despite their mistakes, God was committed to the plan.

Like yours, my own story is still being written. I'm on a journey, and broken dreams are still a reality in that journey. We live in a world of flawed humans who fail us and make mistakes. Many of our dreams are wrapped up in these humans, and because of that, brokenness comes with life on this earth. Despite this reality, I am still experiencing God's better plan. Sometimes I can't even believe the places I've had the opportunity to go to and the friendships I've made along the way. It doesn't seem possible.

> **GOD IS NOT A GOD OF CRUEL TRICKS; HE'S A GOD OF PRECIOUS PROMISES.**

But it is possible! All of it.

The best is truly yet to come if you swap out your own agenda for God's. All of our lives are intertwined in his amazing plan. It's time to wrap your head around the fact that God is going to stay committed to the tomorrow he has in store for you.

This is not another hype man who won't deliver on his word. God is not a god of cruel tricks; he's a God of precious promises.

The promises throughout the Bible are for an abundant life. They are not practical jokes. This amazing tomorrow God has in mind is possible for you and me.

What are we waiting for?

5 TAKEAWAYS

Your dream, the great plan you had, may have failed. Today your life might not look the way you expected. We've established that this can be heartbreaking and discouraging. But your story doesn't have to end there. God has a better dream and plan! As you leave this section of the book, I want to leave you with five action steps to help you step *forward* into your God-given potential.

1. Replace your plan with God's.

   As great as your plan is, you can trust that God has a better one! But receiving this great plan starts with surrendering yours. Such a surrender can feel daunting, but think of it as an exchange and watch what God does.

2. Believe in yourself.

   If you believe in a great God, then it shouldn't be a huge leap to see the greatness that's also in the one he created—*you*. He designed you. You are called, chosen, loved, and gifted (Ephesians 2:10; Philippians 1:6; Zephaniah 3:17; 1 Peter 4:10). If your own failures distract you from this truth, begin reminding yourself of the gifts he has given you.

3. Take a risk.

    It might start with doing a ridiculous thing or two. You may feel scared or embarrassed. But if you don't step out in faith, God can't move! What is one risk you need to take? Write it down, count the cost, then take that risk.

4. Remember that God is on your side.

    The creator of the universe is in your corner. He's rooting for you. He made you, sustains you, and is guiding you down the right path!

    Don't listen to the lie that you are all alone. God has promised, "Never will I leave you; never will I forsake you" (Hebrews 13:5).

5. Listen to the right voice.

    Can you hear him now? God is speaking! He is calling you into the great unknown, the mystery of his will. I don't believe that it's easy to mistake our own thoughts for God's. His voice is clear if you take the time to listen. Lean into his Word, and start making an effort to hear all about his plan for your life.

Part Two
THE QUALIFIED
Who gets to live the dream?

Chapter Three

DEBUNKING THE MYTH

Are you a person who slips the occasional "never" into your statements?

"Oh, that never happens to me."

"I'll never catch a break."

"I'll never land the dream job."

I try to make it a habit not to throw around the word *never* without thinking things through, but the other day I let one slip. I came home to my wife, who was super excited about a dream home she had found in LA. This wasn't just any home; it was a huge house in the perfect spot, everything she had always wanted. It was the kind of house we can't exactly afford at this specific juncture in our lives, but that didn't stop Julia from trying.

"Babe, I bought some raffle tickets for this amazing place in Calabasas!" she yelled with excitement. "We could win the home of our dreams!" She was so pumped to tell me about the contest she had entered so that we could live in this place. In her mind, she had already picked out the curtains and was planning the first party in our new spot.

I couldn't help myself. I immediately shut her down.

"Babe, I never win stuff like this. You basically just threw away our money on those tickets. It's never going to happen." As I watched hope slip away from her excited eyes, I instantly regretted my negative words.

We live in a "never" world. Most people don't believe they could win something big, let alone see the impossible take place in their lives. But people who refuse to use such a limiting word because they're filled with faith for the future are the kind of people who see endless possibilities realized.

When God shows up, we discover that what's impossible for man is possible with him. But far too often people don't believe this statement for themselves. "Well, God doesn't have something special for me, Chad," I've heard some say. "You don't know my family history or my background. You don't know how much I've messed things up for myself. I'm too far gone. I'm not one of those 'super Christians.' Every time I try, I fail."

Many think that if they don't meet a specific set of criteria or fit the perfect mold, they're unqualified and will never walk in what they think of as success or experience the above-and-beyond plans the Bible talks about.

WHAT THE WORLD NULLIFIES, JESUS QUALIFIES.

In Jeremiah 29:11, the prophet wrote, "'For I know the plans I have for you,' declares the LORD, 'plans to prosper you and not to harm you, plans to give you hope and a future.'" The origin of these hopeful plans for the future? God. They are *his* plans that he has for us. The emphasis is on him. The truth is that we can walk in amazing faith and experience our best possible tomorrows because of Jesus and Jesus alone, not because any of us meet a certain set of super-Christian qualifications. This means he can use that terrible past and that failure. What the world nullifies, Jesus qualifies.

ON THE ROAD

The apostle Paul is one of the most famous Christians in history. But when we first meet him in the book of Acts, he's the exact opposite of a model Christian. In fact, he's out to kill all the Christians. We come across him right after the first recorded martyr, Stephen, was stoned to death. There's Paul, standing on the sidelines, cheering everyone on.

But his story really picks up in Acts 9:1. In this portion of Scripture, he is referred to by his Jewish name, Saul. "Meanwhile, Saul was still breathing out murderous threats against the Lord's disciples," the verse says, revealing again how he was not that great of a dude. But then Jesus intervened.

> As he neared Damascus on his journey, suddenly a light from heaven flashed around him. He fell to the ground and heard a voice say to him, "Saul, Saul, why do you persecute me?"
>
> "Who are you, Lord?" Saul asked.
>
> "I am Jesus, whom you are persecuting," he replied. "Now get up and go into the city, and you will be told what you must do." (vv. 3–6)

We're talking about a Christian killer here. In this story where Jesus showed up and changed a life dramatically, Saul was on his way to kill a bunch of innocent people. And God still showed up in the midst of Saul's terrible mission!

Saul's dreams in life prior to this encounter with God were

evil. Because of these evil plans, it's hard for us to believe how the story shifts from here. But from this moment on, everything changed for Saul, later renamed Paul. Because of his encounter with Jesus, he would end up writing the foundation of Christian theology. Luke might have written the largest portions of the New Testament, but Paul would write the books that give us the blueprint on how to live the Christian life. Not only that, but he would also become a great apostle, going into communities and churches, raising up leaders, teaching them about Jesus, and then heading to another town to do it all again.

This man's life is proof that all are qualified to walk in God's plan. He's also proof that you might be on the completely wrong path, heading to do something evil or destructive, and, in a moment, God can change your direction for good.

We serve the type of God who can turn a Christian killer into a church builder. If he can do that, think of all that he can do in your life.

GOD IS PLANNING HIS BEST

In the spring of 2016, we took a trip to Hawaii with my wife's side of the family. We, along with all three of her sisters, their kids, their husbands, and her parents, flew to Maui. Julia's dad had paid for the whole thing as a gift. It was amazing! But with eight children under the age of five, it was also a little chaotic.

While there, my brother-in-law Mort and his wife, Natalie, made plans to take their boys to the beach and then get shaved ice. Scout and Wallace had been playing with their Transformer toys for hours and were enamored with their game, making all the sound effects and doing perfect impressions of Optimus

Prime, when Mort interrupted them. He told them it was time to pack up and go. Immediately, Scout and Wallace freaked out. *How could he tear us away from our Transformers?* they thought. *The nerve!*

They pushed back, but my brother-in-law told them it was time to get in the car and go. He buckled them into their car seats, and as they drove away, Wallace, the younger of the two, said with a pouty lip, "We wish we had a new dad!"

As you can imagine, Mort was heart-broken. He was about to take them to do something even better than what they had been doing! They were going to go body-boarding and hunt for turtles at the beach. They were going to get shaved ice, one of their favorite desserts. He was going to take them to do everything they loved doing! Yes, they had to stop playing with their toys for the moment, but they were on their way to something way better.

> EVEN WHEN WE'RE PLANNING OUR WORST, GOD IS STILL PLANNING HIS BEST.

Sometimes we act this way toward God. We're planning our future, doing the things we dream about, and something gets in our way. Rather than turn to God to ask him what better plan he has for us, we reject him and blame him. We turn into the worst possible version of ourselves. But even when we're planning our worst, God is still planning his best.

Sometimes our dreams aren't bad. For instance, my plan to marry my first serious girlfriend wasn't evil, but God had something better in mind. My nephews' plan to play with their Transformers wasn't bad either, but if they had kept playing, they would have missed out on their dad's better plan.

Sometimes our current dreams or the dreams of our past *are* bad. They might even be fueled by sin, for instance lust or a greedy desire. In Acts 9, Paul was on his way to kill, steal, and destroy. If most of us had met him at this particular moment in his journey, we would've probably turned our backs on him. We don't want to be around those who behave badly. We reject gossipers, liars, slanderers, killers, and haters. We don't easily forgive those who do evil. Luckily for us, God doesn't react the way we do. Even in these instances, when we're following our not-so-holy desires, God figures out a way to bring his plan together for us. Paul schemed to do evil, but God still worked out a way to get him on the path he had mapped out for him. Even when our choices are taking us in the wrong direction, God holds on to the plan he's written for our lives.

God is not like a man, and he doesn't view us the way we view ourselves. He's a heavenly father. He's a father like my brother-in-law, who still took his sons to the beach and gave them an amazing day even though they had completely rejected him in the car. Even though Paul was rebelling against everything God was doing, God still believed in his potential and didn't let anything disqualify him from walking in it.

WHY WAIT?

After Paul, then still called Saul, encountered Jesus, he got up off the ground, opened his eyes, and saw . . . nothing. Blind, he traveled to Damascus. Again, planning for Paul's best, God went before him and spoke to a man named Ananias. The Bible tells it this way in Acts 9:10–12:

In Damascus there was a disciple named Ananias. The Lord called to him in a vision, "Ananias!"

"Yes, Lord," he answered.

The Lord told him, "Go to the house of Judas on Straight Street and ask for a man from Tarsus named Saul, for he is praying. In a vision he has seen a man named Ananias come and place his hands on him to restore his sight."

It would be Ananias's job to lay hands on Saul and pray that his blindness would be healed. Ananias's reply to God went a little something like this: "Hold up. You mean the Christian-killer guy? The one who was there when Stephen was stoned? The guy we're all afraid of?"

Ananias said, "Lord . . . I have heard many reports about this man and all the harm he has done to your holy people in Jerusalem. And he has come here with authority from the chief priests to arrest all who call on your name" (v. 13).

"Really, God? Really? He's not qualified to live out your plan. He's not the guy I'd choose to heal or use" is what Ananias was really saying in response to the Lord's request.

Ananias believed the myth that you have to look and act a certain way to live out God's great plan. But despite his reservations, the disciple was obedient, and God used him to bring back Saul's sight. God also used him to tell Saul about the Jesus who had met him on the road.

I love the next part of the story. Right after Ananias told Saul about Jesus, after Saul learned just a little bit of information about this Christianity thing, and after he got saved in Acts 9, Scripture says, "Immediately, something like scales fell from Saul's eyes, and he could see again" (v. 18). God healed Saul just like he said he would. But the story doesn't end there. It continues, saying, "He got up and was baptized, and after taking some food, he regained his strength" (vv. 18–19).

Saul was healed, refreshed, and baptized. He was like new again and back to his old, healthy self. What would you do next? I would probably take a nap and recover from the whole being-blinded-by-God thing. Not Saul, though.

Verses 19–20 describe Saul's next move: "Saul spent several days with the disciples in Damascus. At once he began to preach in the synagogues that *Jesus is the Son of God*" (emphasis added).

Wait, what?

At once, he was healed.

At once, he went and got baptized.

And what's most amazing of all?

At once, he began to preach Christ! Dude didn't mess around.

This means one day Paul was out killing Christians, and then "several days" later he was preaching Jesus. That's like one Saturday he's in the club selling drugs, and the next Sunday he's preaching God on the platform.

This doesn't make sense to most of us. You can't just go from killing to preaching. We tend to think you need to take a timeout and work on stuff before moving forward. Maybe Paul should've gone to Christian Killers Anonymous for a few weeks. He should've probably completed the program, gone to a rehab center, or spent some time in jail, and then maybe, just maybe, we could hand him a mic and put a Bible in his hands.

But that's not the way God is. God's not looking for perfect people who fit a specific mold to walk into his plan. He looked at someone like Saul and asked, "Why wait? Let's do this now! This guy is willing. He's ready. He believes in me. He has the faith. Let's make this tomorrow happen!"

> **GOD'S NOT LOOKING FOR YOUR CAPABILITY; HE'S LOOKING FOR YOUR AVAILABILITY.**

When it comes to your future, God's not looking for your capability; he's looking for your availability. Maybe you're ignoring the plan because you think it's only for "them" and not for you. Maybe your problem is not that God hasn't chosen you or that your past is too messed up, but that you're too busy waiting to get perfectly right with him before you think you can be used.

When I was just a young youth minister, fresh out of Bible college, I had zero qualifications for the job. I remember the first time I had to preach. I was so nervous. *What was I thinking? I thought. I shouldn't be doing this!* As I drove to the church, I blasted Tupac in the car to pump myself up. Now, if that doesn't demonstrate how unprepared I was to be preaching to young people, I don't know what does. But, in the end, I trusted that God would use my quirks and mistakes and just kept moving forward. And you know what? Despite my personal insecurities and inappropriate choice of musical inspiration, God *did* use me.

You might think that you need textbook preparedness and perfection to step into God's will, but with this perspective, you could be waiting your whole life to walk in your future. I'm glad I didn't wait until I had my act together to preach my first sermon. I would still be waiting today!

It's time to stop waiting for the supposedly perfect conditions.

God doesn't need you to be perfect. He needs you to show up with faith and a little bit of fiery passion. He needs you to say, "What do you have for me next? I'm ready." This is what he saw in Paul: a passionate person who was channeling his passion in the wrong way. And he used this passionate man for good. He didn't ask him to tone it down once he got saved. Instead, God used his unique personality. He was the one who made Paul that way. And he made him that way for a reason, just like he made you the way you are for a reason.

> **WHAT IF IT'S OUR INADEQUACIES, NOT OUR ACHIEVEMENTS, THAT MAKE US THE PERFECT CANDIDATES?**

Step away from yourself and examine your own life. Ask yourself, "How did God create me? What part of my unique design is he asking me to make available for him to use?" What if it's our inadequacies, not our achievements, that make us the perfect candidates?

LEAVE THE PAST IN THE PAST

It's one thing to realize that God has an amazing plan for us despite our flaws and failures, and it's another to actually walk in this belief. It's no easy task to release ourselves from the mistakes and embarrassments of our past. Again, let's look at Paul to see how he handled things.

If anyone should've felt disqualified, it was Paul. He could've spent his life dwelling on the mistakes of his evil dreams, the people he murdered, and the hate he spread. But instead he traveled to cities, preaching Christianity, and is still quoted throughout the world today. Because he was obsessed with Jesus, the object of our faith, he didn't let his history keep him from walking out God's future. And he embraced his weaknesses and his disqualifications. After all, these were what highlighted how great and redeeming God truly is. He expanded on this thought in his letter to the Corinthians, saying, "If I must boast, I will boast of the things that show my weakness" (2 Corinthians 11:30). He is also known for saying that "Christ Jesus came into the world to save sinners—of whom I am the worst" (1 Timothy 1:15).

Though he's no apostle Paul, I like the way Michael Jordan sums up this thought about the failures of his past. "I've missed more than 9,000 shots in my career. I've lost almost 300 games. Twenty-six times, I've been trusted to take the game-winning shot and missed. I've failed over and over and over again in my life. And that is why I succeed."

So many of us dwell on our past, our weaknesses, and the times we missed the shots we took. We think being "the worst" means we're out of the game, removed from the plan for good. We ask, "How do you get over an abortion?" "How do you get over an affair?" "How do you get over losing at your dream?"

We've gone places. We've touched things. We've done dark, evil things. *How do I get over something like this and step into my God-given potential?*

Paul put it this way in Philippians 3:12–14:

I press on to take hold of that for which Christ Jesus took hold of me. Brothers and sisters, I do not consider myself yet to have taken hold of it. But one thing I do: Forgetting what is behind and straining toward what is ahead, I press on toward the goal to win the prize for which God has called me heavenward in Christ Jesus.

It's time to forget about the imperfections that are behind us, all those mistakes and regrets, and step into God's perfect future for our lives. If God can help Paul get over the emotional baggage that comes with murdering innocent people and move on to preaching the faith, you can move forward too.

But how?

Start with writing down one thing that's holding you back. Maybe it's a mistake you've made; maybe it's a failure in a certain area of your life. Fill in the blank:

Because I've done _____, I have trouble doing _____.

Once it's written down, throw that piece of paper in the trash can. Burn it if you need to. This is how Jesus sees your past. It's forgotten. Because of him, you don't have to let these issues hold you back.

After letting go of this thing, you have to make your future about the one who created you, the one who has mapped out a promising tomorrow for you. Paul was pressing "on toward the goal" of Christ Jesus. He could transform from Christian killer to church builder because of this goal.

> **STOP LIVING DISQUALIFIED; KNOW THAT YOU'VE BEEN JUSTIFIED.**

It's time to stop letting your past and misconceptions of what it means to be qualified delay your destiny. Watch what happens when you start making every step you take about Jesus, the one who made you right before God despite your failures. Stop living disqualified; know that you've been justified. You'll soon discover the road that leads to everlasting, abundant life. You'll soon walk in this plan we're talking about.

Chapter Four

"I WANT YOUR HEART, NOT YOUR PERFECTION"

I woke up, rolled over, and grabbed my phone.

Before brushing my teeth, washing my face, or drinking a cup of coffee, I picked up the little device that holds my world. Without even realizing I'd tapped my way there, I was suddenly staring at Instagram.

I didn't stop to wonder how I'd gotten to this place. I didn't stop to ponder what the habit of checking social media first thing in the morning says about the state of our world. Not a thought passed through my mind as my thumb instantly started scrolling. I was operating on automatic. Barely even coherent, I began stalking the world outside my warm, cozy bed.

I saw photos from the party the night before. I wondered why I wasn't invited.

I saw my friend wearing that jacket I wanted. I tried to shove down my small hatred of all the old jackets that hung in my closet.

I saw another friend eating a healthy breakfast. I decided it was time to start that habit up again. I instantly remembered the peanut M&M's I'd crushed the night before.

Another photo.

And another.

People were looking good. They were looking really good.

I glanced at the clock on my phone. I had been doing this for ten whole minutes, just staring at people in their best clothes with their best smiles eating the best food.

I decided to finally get up and brush my teeth.

ONLY THE BEST

Today we live in a world where everything is about us. Because of social media, we're all constantly working on our brand. We take photos and write captions that tell others how to view us. And these photos typically involve us looking our best, with the hope that others believe we're always at our best.

You hop on your phone, look at a photo of your friends at a party, and think, *These people look amazing!* Like the morning I described above, sometimes this can make me look at my own life and feel less than. But other times I'm just plain entertained. I've even invented a little guessing game I call, "How many filters did they put on this one?"

I'll look at a picture and try to figure out if they've thrown it in Snapseed, filtered it up, and then gone over to VSCO and filtered it up again. See if I can tell if they've even added some contrast when they put it into the IG.

All this filtering and editing and contrasting makes for one beautiful-looking photo . . .

. . . of complete strangers.

Sometimes I'm scratching my head, wondering if I actually know this person I'm following. Then I'll see their username and realize it's someone I had seen just a few days earlier and they look nothing like the image in my feed.

This tendency to filter until we're unrecognizable comes from the human desire to show others only our very best. We want people to see how good we are and how awesome we look, even if it's far from reality. Fear of rejection produces fake perfection.

FEAR OF REJECTION PRODUCES FAKE PERFECTION.

This habit becomes a problem, particularly when we apply it to our relationship with God. We're so used to doctoring up a representation of our lives that we feel we can only come to God with our very best. We want to feel put together when we pray or show up at church. When we ask, "Who gets to live the dream?" we tend to answer with, "Only the most perfect of Christians" or "Only those who haven't failed miserably."

Maybe this isn't your exact answer, but if you stop to think about it, you may realize this underlying mind-set often plays into the way you approach God.

The reality is that the "qualified" people God uses look more like a ragtag group of the beaten and broken than impressive images of perfection. They look like people "boasting" in their faults, flaws, shattered goals, and mistakes of the past. Because it's these qualities that showcase God's goodness.

God is not looking for our best; he's more interested in our weakness. He's not asking for us to follow him and walk out his plan only after we've become completely perfect. He wants us to stretch out the things that need him most—the ugly, broken parts of our lives—and offer them to him. And he wants us to do it with faith.

We try to hide our ugliness from God just as we hide the parts of ourselves we are ashamed of from others. I remember one summer it was hot, and we were over at our friend's pool trying to cool off. A few hours into the swim, some more people showed up. I had never met these new people, but they parked themselves in lawn chairs near the pool, and we all began chatting. It's always a little awkward when half the group is in swimming suits and the rest are fully clothed, but I embraced the awkwardness and joined the group sitting in lawn chairs.

While talking with them, I suddenly looked down and noticed my feet. Have you ever glanced down at your toes and felt like you hadn't given them a good, hard look in a long time? They were not well taken care of. In fact, they looked pretty gross. And I started to panic.

> IT'S WHEN WE COME TO THE END OF OURSELVES THAT WE COME TO THE BEGINNING WITH GOD.

Everyone in the group was shooting the breeze, unaware of the eyesore just a glance away. People were getting to know each other, the fully clothed telling stories to the swimsuit-clad. We were all laughing and enjoying our time. And I was there, putting on my best fake laugh, as I slyly pulled a towel over my feet to hide my disgrace.

For the rest of the day, I stayed in that position with the towel covering my toes.

"We're gonna go get a drink inside. You want to join?" they asked.

"No, I'm good here!" I lied. All I could think about was how to hide my nasty toes from these people.

Because of shame and fear, we all try to hide the thing we think is most unappealing about ourselves, whether that be the mistakes of our past, our dark side, or our inabilities, from God. Just as we fear our Instagram friends will judge us or unfriend us, we're scared that God may withhold his love and amazing plan from us if he knows what we really look like. When we're going through things as difficult as depression, addiction, losing our job, failing at our dreams, or ending a relationship, the last thing we want to do is bring these struggles to God. But it's when we come to the end of ourselves that we come to the beginning with God.

HE SEES ME AS I'M SUPPOSED TO BE

Psalms 139:16 says, "Your eyes saw my unformed body; all the days ordained for me were written in your book before one of them came to be." God doesn't look at us shallowly like man does. You might be in the middle of your struggle, in a lowly state, but that's not where God sees you. He sees your "unformed substance," the person you are meant to be.

Too many of us are caught up in our imperfections, while God is caught up in our future selves. He's not looking at us the way those around us are, seeing only our messes, our situations, our struggles, and our weaknesses. He sees us as something far greater. Where we see "unworthy," "undeserving," and "unqualified," God sees the opposite. He sees his dream team.

The author of those words in Psalm 139 was David, and his origin story paints a beautiful picture of the way God views each of us. Before David became a godly man and mighty king, God spoke to the prophet Samuel about him. At the time, Israel had a king named Saul, and things weren't exactly working out. So God told the prophet, "How long will you mourn for Saul, since I have rejected him as king of Israel? Fill your horn with oil and be on your way; I am sending you to Jesse of Bethlehem. I have chosen one of his sons to be king" (1 Samuel 16:1).

Samuel did what God told him and traveled to Bethlehem to find this new king among Jesse's sons. When he arrived at Jesse's house, Jesse lined up all his strapping young boys in front of Samuel. I always imagine that Jesse marched them out with a big grin on his face, so proud of the young men he had raised. I also imagine Samuel, pacing back and forth among them, sizing them all up. In my head, the whole thing is like the rose ceremony at the end of an episode of *The Bachelor*. Who would walk away with the rose and become the next king of Israel?

The first son was probably the smart, Google-employee type of guy. You know, the one who always has the answers to everything. Samuel looked him up and down.

"Nope. Not the Google guy."

I picture the next one as more of a Gronkowski type. He was the athlete, all brawn. Samuel gave him a good, hard look.

"Meh. Not the Gronk."

Maybe the third was the good-looking one, the one with a modeling career on the side. The Zoolander of Bethlehem.

"Nope. Not the model kid."

After he went through all the sons and was greatly discouraged, Samuel finally looked at Jesse and said, "None of these is the guy I'm looking for. Do you have any more sons?"

"Well . . ."

Jesse had shrugged off one of his boys, thinking him

unimportant to Samuel's quest. Because of this son's current state, because he was young and insignificant, Jesse had neglected to bring out David, his youngest.

Verse 11 says when Samuel asked if there were any more sons, Jesse answered, "There is still the youngest. . . . He is tending the sheep."

David wasn't the Google employee, the Gronk, or Zoolander. To Jesse, he didn't seem to matter much at all. But Samuel knew.

"Send for him," Samuel said when he learned there was one more.

David arrived, and Samuel knew instantly that David was the one he had come for. He was the great future leader God had promised. How did he know this? Before David got there, God had spoken these words to the old prophet: "The Lord does not look at the things people look at. People look at the outward appearance, but the Lord looks at the heart" (v. 7).

The moment David walked in, Samuel knew what God had meant by these words. God was not looking for the model or the athlete. He didn't care about what man cared about.

It's because of this contrast between what God is looking for and what man is looking for that Samuel was in this situation in the first place. Saul, the king before David, was chosen by the Israelites because he was tall, dark, and handsome. He fit the mold to a T. The Bible even calls him as "handsome a young man as could be found anywhere in Israel" (1 Samuel 9:2). But God couldn't have cared less about Saul's Instagram-filter game, his achievements, or his ability to seem perfect to man. He knew that his heart was not what Israel needed.

God saw David and, despite his youth, said, "This is a king." He saw Peter, though he failed at his job and God knew he would one day deny him three times, and said, "This is a rock." He saw Paul, murdering Christians and doing evil, and said, "I'm going to spread Christianity with this man." Just as he saw all these flawed people, he sees where you're supposed to be one day.

Throughout the Bible, Jesus interacted with the unimpressive, even the disastrous. We see him mightily use tax collectors like Matthew, people society hated. Tax collectors were known for cheating those around them, and yet Jesus chose Matthew as one of his twelve. And then Matthew would go on to write one of the four gospels.

We also see Jesus stand up for an adulterous woman in front of the scribes. John 8:1–11 tells the story of this woman who should've been stoned for her sin. When the scribes asked what they should do to her, Jesus answered with, "Let any one of you who is without sin be the first to throw a stone at her" (v. 7). Jesus didn't have to stick up for this woman! She had gone against the rules of the Law that God had written. She had sinned. She deserved death. But this is who he chose to defend.

> **HE'S NOT LOOKING AT YOUR OUTWARD ACCOMPLISHMENT BUT AT YOUR INWARD ACKNOWLEDGMENT.**

It's clear that it's not a perfect track record or super-Christian powers God is checking off on his list. He loves you just the way you are and is ready to use you for his great purposes. He's not looking at your outward accomplishment but at your inward acknowledgment. It's a pure heart he's after. The Bible describes David as a "man after [God's] own heart" (Acts 13:22). David was completely in love with God and full of faith, and you can see it throughout his story and in his psalms. And at the end of the day, that's all God is looking for.

YOU BELONG

Have you ever shown up at a place and instantly felt like you didn't belong there?

When I first moved to LA, I remember feeling this emotion strongly when my friend took me out to a hip restaurant. I looked around at all the young, the rich, and the famous and thought, *I do not belong here. I don't dress like these people. I'm definitely not as cool as these people.* I felt inferior and was ready to turn around and walk right out the door.

For many of us, confidence is a by-product of belonging. When we walk into a room and feel like we fit in with the people and surroundings, our attitude shifts. Insecurity and shame are instantly replaced with energy and excitement.

David, chosen by God despite his flaws, knew what it felt like to go from the shame of not belonging, not being invited to the table, to the joy of being called into God's plan, the ultimate belonging. And he didn't keep this experience to himself.

Let's look at David's story again. Eventually he would become the king of Israel, just as God planned. After years of turmoil with Saul, David finally took the throne. Because of his position, he lived a life of prosperity. Every night he'd sit at the most epic of banqueting tables and have his choice of steak, cheese, bread, and wine. Forget Chick-fil-A. This was a *feast*. David knew what it meant to belong and have a seat at the banqueting table.

But long before all this came to pass, this shepherd boy had a best friend named Jonathan, who was Saul's son. These two were like high school BFFs—nicknames, friendship bracelets, and all. When war with the Philistines, Israel's enemy, ultimately led to the death of Saul and his sons, David didn't just say good-bye to the trouble he'd endured with the king; he also lost his close friend. And so, before he was anointed king, David mourned for Jonathan.

One day, after David had been ruling for a while, he got a crazy idea in his head. In 2 Samuel 9, it says that David asked, "Is there anyone still left of the house of Saul to whom I can show kindness for Jonathan's sake?" (v. 1, author's paraphrase).

He basically asked one of the servants to hop on Google and see if any member of Jonathan's family was alive. So one of the servants started searching away and discovered that there was one family member still around: Jonathan's son Mephibosheth.

Let's just pause the story right here. What kind of parent names his child Mephibosheth? How does a kid even learn to spell a name like that?

To make the name worse, its meaning is "from the mouth of shame." This is because Mephibosheth was his family's disgrace. Because he was crippled, with two lame feet, they hid him away from the world. David had never heard of him prior to that moment. Mephibosheth's name served as a constant reminder of the shame he caused his entire family.

Mephibosheth was the last person you'd ever think to see in a king's court. A blemish to his family, Mephibosheth probably never felt like he belonged anywhere. David discovered that Mephibosheth lived in the city of Lo Debar. What's fascinating is

that this city's name means "no communication," further showing how cut off Mephibosheth was from the world.

Many of us can relate to Mephibosheth. The young boy had
no part in the nation of Israel or the big decisions that David was
making for God. We might feel the same way about our own
lives. Our destructive thinking takes the form of comparing
ourselves to others, and because of our inadequacies, we think
the line of communication with God has been completely sev-
ered. But Mephibosheth's story doesn't end in Lo Debar, and
ours doesn't have to end in the land of no communication either.

David knew that despite where he lived and his condition,
this boy was a part of Jonathan's family. This was his closest
friend's son. He couldn't continue life locked away from the
rest of the world. And so, David did something surprising when
he made this discovery. Verse 5 says, "King David didn't lose a
minute. He sent and got him" (THE MESSAGE).

He didn't wait one more moment. Once he knew about
Jonathan's son, he asked the servants to find him and bring him
to the courts. He didn't care that he was crippled or tucked away
from the world! So he sent for him and Mephibosheth came:
"When Mephibosheth son of Jonathan (who was the son of Saul),
came before David, he bowed deeply, abasing himself, honoring
David" (v. 6 THE MESSAGE).

Used to a life of shame, Mephibosheth felt completely un-
worthy. So unworthy that he abased himself in front of David.
Just as we are often reluctant to come before God in our weakness, Mephibosheth was embarrassed to be seen in such a
glorious place. I love David's response here. It also reminds me
of our relationship with God. The story goes on this way:

David spoke his name: "Mephibosheth."

"Yes sir?"

"Don't be frightened," said David. "I'd like to do something special for you in memory of your father Jonathan. To begin with, I'm returning to you all the properties of your grandfather Saul. Furthermore, from now on you'll take all your meals at my table."

Shuffling and stammering, not looking him in the eye, Mephibosheth said, "Who am I that you pay attention to a stray dog like me?" (vv. 6–8 THE MESSAGE)

All Mephibosheth had ever known were his imperfections. He saw himself as nothing, "a stray dog," even! But David did the unthinkable. He gave him property and a seat at his table. David didn't care that he couldn't walk. He didn't care that he was the shame of his family. David only knew that he loved Jonathan and, therefore, loved Jonathan's family. David's invitation showed Mephibosheth that, though he was considered a blemish by the world, and even by his own family, he still belonged.

This moving story demonstrates the love of God. No matter what you've done or who you are, he wants greatness for you. He invites you to epic, awe-inspiring places, and he says, "You belong at my table."

How differently would you view yourself if you knew you belonged? Maybe you're like Mephibosheth, unable to walk into God's plan because you're so ashamed of your weakness and the dreams that didn't pan out the way you had hoped. God is saying it's not your flaws that qualify you. It's his love!

WHERE DO WE GO FROM HERE?

If we don't have to be perfect to walk into God's amazing plan, and we can bring the ugliest parts of ourselves—our shame, our failures, and our weaknesses—to him, now what? Do we simply keep walking in this shame and ugliness? Though we belong even if we've made the worst of mistakes, do we continue to make those mistakes? If we're maimed and crippled, should we still believe that's the way it will always be for us?

Absolutely not!

As you begin to realize that God's amazing plans are even for the imperfect, you'll also need to realize one important fact: God loves you just the way you are, but he loves you way too much to leave you that way.

We're all grateful that Jesus loves, accepts, and forgives even the greatest of sinners. But he doesn't stop there. When you finally understand that you belong and choose to walk in faith, you'll begin to see God's transforming power.

He comes into our lives and instantly begins to rearrange things. Jesus healed so many throughout the Bible, like the crippled beggar in John 5, the woman with the issue of blood in Mark 5, and the blind man in John 9. Just as he gave the crippled back his legs, freed the woman of her infirmities, and restored vision to the blind, Jesus is ready to heal whatever issue, limp, or hurt you bring to him.

Your broken marriage isn't too far gone for Jesus. The anxiety you struggle with doesn't intimidate him. The dream you tried and failed won't embarrass him. He's ready to use and heal all your messes. It starts by coming to him with a sense of belonging. Approach him in prayer throughout the day, and think about his plan with a new perspective—one that knows nothing is impossible with him.

God's plan is to make you and your future even better than it is right now, but first you must realize that you belong in that future and be ready to bring your weakness to him.

Chapter Five

MAKE NO MISTAKE

Have you ever gone the wrong way on a one-way street? I typically try to avoid driving in downtown LA because there is nothing more terrifying than driving along a city street, making a turn, and realizing there's a car coming straight toward you.

There's usually that awkward moment when you realize you can't pull over because cars are parked on either side of the lane. This is when you put your car in reverse and back down the street while giving a lingering apologetic look to the driver who is facing you.

We've all experienced wrong-turn moments in life. Sometimes this looks like a bad investment, a broken relationship, or a blowup that you later regret. When it comes to mistakes in my life, the area I need the most improvement in is my marriage.

I remember Julia's and my first Christmas together. I wish I could report it was full of only warm, fuzzy moments, but that wasn't our reality. We were on vacation with my parents in Coeur d'Alene, Idaho. Poor Julia was only three months into our marriage, taking birth control pills for the first time, and dealing with an intense hormonal reaction, and she had to spend Christmas miles away from her family.

Things didn't start off well. We were driving along in the car together, my mom, Julia, and me. Suddenly, a fight broke out. Julia and Mama Veach were not getting along. I started to sweat, looking back and forth between the two nervously. This was not how Christmas was supposed to play out.

Finally, I decided to speak up. I did what any new husband would do when faced with such adversity . . .

I took my mom's side.

I can almost feel you cringing as you hold this book. I can sense your eyebrows raising. I know what you're saying to yourself at this moment: *What were you thinking, Chad?!*

Rather than approach the situation with empathy, I made a huge mistake. Julia felt immediately alone, and it affected the rest of the trip. Christmas was ruined. I made a terrible wrong turn.

A while later, Julia sat me down and told me how I had failed her. She'd needed me in that car. I was filled with regret. I had let down the most important person in my life. We made a decision from that moment forward to be more gracious to each other and to always have each other's backs no matter what.

I wish I could say I always get it right. It's definitely been a process. But despite my constant failings, Julia hasn't given up on me or the dream of our marriage. Even when my mistakes are huge, they don't take me out of the equation.

Many times people feel that the mistakes they've made along the road of their lives disqualify them from walking in God's dream. They think one wrong turn makes them un-worthy of anything good, and they believe that once they've taken that wrong turn on a one-way street, they can't correct their course.

God knows exactly where he's leading each of us; he always has a plan for us even if we're lost and completely unaware of that plan or have made blunders along the way. Whether we believe it for ourselves or not, God believes in us.

> **GOD WILL NARROW OUR OPTIONS UNTIL HE'S OUR ONLY OPTION.**

And the beautiful thing about his grace is that he's committed to his plan for us, even if we mess things up for ourselves. Oftentimes, even when we get on the wrong path, God will narrow our options until he's our only option.

HE'LL CALL YOU

We've talked about the life of Mephibosheth and how God had a plan despite Mephibosheth's weaknesses. We've examined the life of Paul and seen that even though he'd committed evil acts, God still had a future for him. Now let's look at the life of Jonah.

Before we dive into this story, a little history lesson: At the time this story took place, the people of Nineveh were some of Israel's most hated enemies. They were known for violence and extreme acts of evil. Every part of their culture was against God. You have to understand this to have empathy for Jonah's situation.

Jonah 1:1–3 says:

The word of the LORD came to Jonah son of Amittai: "Go to

the great city of Nineveh and preach against it, because its wickedness has come up before me."

But Jonah ran away from the LORD and headed for Tarshish. He went down to Joppa, where he found a ship bound for that port. After paying the fare, he went aboard and sailed for Tarshish to flee from the LORD.

At the very start of this book, we see the grace of God in his treatment of Nineveh. Even though the city was full of wickedness, God still had a plan to share the good news with the people there. This sets the stage for the same kindness God would extend toward Jonah later in the story.

As we can see from the passage above, Jonah made a mistake right off the bat. God said, "I want you to go to Nineveh," and Jonah's reaction went a little something like this:

"Nineveh? This time of year? Peace. I'm out!"

It wasn't that Jonah's dream was broken and God showed him a better one; it was that Jonah didn't want God's dream. He thought *God's* plan was the broken one. Sometimes we try our own thing, and then only in our failure do we turn to God. Other times we flat-out reject the dream God is trying to show us. Rather than say, "God doesn't have a plan for me," Jonah said, "God told me his plan, and I don't want any part of it."

I'm sure Jonah was wondering, *Does he even know what he's asking of me?* He probably felt like he was being thrown to the lions or that God had some sort of death wish for him.

"That's great and all," Jonah probably said to himself, "but I don't like Nineveh. I've never been to Nineveh. I have no plans to ever go to Nineveh. Everyone knows that place is evil and awful. Not cool, God. Not cool."

So he disobeyed God and fled in the exact opposite direction. He completely defied God's plans and paid the fare to Tarshish.

Before moving on, let's stop at this point in the story. The fact that "the word of the LORD came to Jonah" reveals how God wants to work in each of our lives. God rings us up. He comes into our space. He'll talk directly to our hearts. This is how he reveals his plan. He is the initiator of the plan. If you think you're the one starting this thing, you're greatly mistaken. Just as God initiated the great plan for salvation through Jesus, he initiates his plan for each of us.

Did you know that you didn't find God, but God found you? You weren't pursuing him; he was pursuing you. Why? Because he loves you and wants you to walk in your potential. This is what he did with Jonah. God looked at him and said, "I have great things in store for this one." He had authored and planned for Jonah to bring the good news of God's grace and kindness to a doomed people. And so he came to Jonah to tell him all about it.

And he'll come to you too. You might be wondering, *When he comes, how will I know that it's God who's really speaking to me? How will I know that it's him when he brings the word about my plan?* Many have a difficult time discerning the difference between their own voices and God's voice. But Jesus said, "My sheep recognize my voice" (John 10:27 THE MESSAGE). If we're following him, we will be able to recognize when it's God asking us to do something.

This recognition feels similar to when you're watching an animated movie and recognize the voice of an actor. The last one I saw in the theater with my family was *Finding Dory*. Right in the middle of the movie, this beluga character came onto the screen, and everything paused for me. Instantly, I thought, *I know that voice. Who is that voice?*

I refused to Google it right then and there, but I probably spent a good third of the movie straining to solve the puzzle.

I know it. Who is that?!

Finally, after I missed pretty much the entire plot, it came to me.

The dad from *Modern Family*!

I was yelling and cheering inside my head. Everyone there thought I was watching the movie the whole time like they were, but in reality I was throwing a little party for myself. *What sweet relief!*

It may sound strange, but hearing God's voice is a lot like that. There's something about the sound that clicks inside of you. You know where it's coming from. You recognize it, because it's God. If you're worried about not being able to discern it or concerned you'll miss the big moment, remember that heaven doesn't sound like your own internal monologue. In fact, sometimes its prompting sounds like something you'd never in a million years think of doing on your own.

WILL YOU PAY THE FARE TO GET ON THE SHIP OF BLESSING OR ON THE SHIP OF BURDEN?

God called Jonah. "Jonah! It's me! I'm bringing you to reach this city. I have such great plans for you! You're going to help save these people, Jonah! Let's do this."

Jonah's problem was not that he didn't recognize God's voice. He heard the call and knew where it was coming from, but rather than obeying, he deliberately, intentionally paid the fare to sail in the opposite direction. He didn't want to travel to the city of his enemies. He didn't want to share the news about God's love and grace with people he feared and disliked. He was more into *his* dreams than God's. So he made the wrong choice.

God *will* call you. He will speak to you about his plans, but it's up to you to walk them out. If you choose to defy his plan, you'll carry the burden of your mistake and rebellion. Will you pay the fare to get on the ship of blessing or on the ship of burden?

YOU CAN ALWAYS CALL ON GOD

Jonah, like many of us, made a huge mistake. His mistake came in the form of deliberately disobeying God. Your mistakes might look a little different. Maybe you've lied to get ahead in this world; maybe you've cheated and hurt the people around you; maybe you've developed some bad habits and addictions. Mistake makers are not alone in this world. We all make mistakes. Because of Jonah's mistake, the next part of his story took a dark turn. "Then the LORD sent a great wind on the sea, and such a violent storm arose that the ship threatened to break up" (Jonah 1:4).

This storm was so aggressive that the fishermen on the boat noticed something was wrong. They were trying to discover who was responsible for this calamity (v. 7). They knew this wasn't any ordinary storm. This storm was caused by someone's wrongdoing. Somebody was to blame. Jonah in his rebellion had made the rain, wind, and waves come. I think most of us have been in a similar boat. It's one thing to experience a trying season of life, like a health issue or a death in your family. It's quite another thing when your storm or trial is your own fault.

Sometimes the wrong decisions we make on the way to our

dreams, or the things we do when we try to accomplish something our way, lead to our destruction and even threaten the destruction of those around us. And sometimes it's by God's grace that there even is a storm. Often, storms we face are not to hurt us but to help us. They cause our choices to narrow until all we have left is God. He's ready to intercede in our worst moments so that he can get our attention. And God uses all of this to lead us to his great plan for each of our lives.

Jonah's story continues with the fishermen as they, like the good friends that they were, drew straws to figure out who was causing all the trouble and threw Jonah overboard. Then, the Scriptures say, "the LORD provided a huge fish to swallow Jonah, and Jonah was in the belly of the fish three days and three nights" (v. 17).

It's while he was in the belly of the fish that Jonah finally called out to God. "In my distress I called to the LORD, and he answered me. From deep in the realm of the dead I called for help, and you listened to my cry" (2:2).

I picture Jonah pacing back and forth inside that fish, talking to himself. We all like to talk to ourselves like crazy people now and again, right? Maybe you're like me and are super sarcastic with yourself when you mess things up.

"Oh, good job, Chad! You've really *done* it now! Aren't you proud of yourself? Do you like how this worked out? Huh, genius?"

Or maybe you take the beating-yourself-up approach. "You are so stupid! Stupid! Stupid!"

I bet Jonah was shouting in the fish, "You're in a fish now, buddy. You happy about that? Well, are you?"

No matter what wrong decisions you've made or detours you've taken on your journey with God, it's never too late to lift up your voice to him. Jonah realized in the belly of the fish that he had messed up; he had done the exact opposite of God's will. You might be realizing, "I messed up my marriage," "I hurt my family," "I looked at something I never should have," "I went too far," "I said dishonest words," or "I did something I said I would never do again." Jonah's story is evidence that these kinds of missteps don't disqualify you from God's dream for your life.

When we're asking the question, "Who gets to walk in this plan?" we can look at Jonah's story to discover who this includes. Even those who have gone the wrong way are part of this "who." Even those who rejected God's plan can turn around and repent. No matter what we've done, we can always call on God and reach his listening ears. "In my distress I called to the LORD. I cried to my God for help. From his temple he heard my voice; my cry came before him, into his ears" (Psalm 18:6).

As a father of three children, I know when one of my babies is crying and whose voice it is. When my youngest, Mav, starts whimpering, I know instantly that it's baby Mav. When Georgia's wailing, I know, "That's my Georgia. She needs me." When Winston cries, I know that it's Winston and that it's way too early in the morning for him to be crying. (Help me, Lord Jesus, with that child's sleep patterns.)

Just as a father knows each of his children's unique voices, God knows your voice. He won't cover his ears and ignore his children even if we've done him wrong or disobeyed. He won't erase us from the plan he's already written.

Instead, he moves toward us, ready to listen and step in when we call out to him.

THE GOD OF SECOND CHANCES

What happens when we mess things up for ourselves? Does God turn his back on us and go with a contingency plan? In the book of Jonah, we see a storm and a fish that swallows our hero alive, but the story doesn't end there. Jonah 3:1 says, "Then the word of the LORD came to Jonah a second time."

> **IF YOU DON'T GET IT RIGHT THE FIRST TIME, GOD WILL ALWAYS GIVE YOU A SECOND CHANCE.**

I believe if you don't get it right the first time, God will always give you a second chance. God heard Jonah's cry and again told him about his big plan. "Go to the great city of Nineveh and proclaim to it the message I give you" (v. 2).

And after the second time, "Jonah obeyed the word of the LORD and went to Nineveh" (v. 3). It took God coming twice with a word about the plan for Jonah to finally get his act together. God was gracious enough to give him another shot. But I believe that even if Jonah had fled again, God would have stepped in and given him a third, fourth, fifth, even hundredth chance. It's like the bottomless fries at Red Robin; there's no end to God's grace.

Jesus demonstrated this when Peter asked him how many times he should forgive someone who sinned against him (Matthew 18). Peter, being a good Jew, knew that the old law said to forgive someone up to seven times. Each person would get seven chances and then . . . strike! They were out. But Peter had been hanging out with Jesus for a while at this point and was probably getting a sense that the new law and way of doing things were a bit different from what he'd grown up learning. I'm sure he wasn't surprised when Jesus answered his question with this extreme: "I tell you, not seven times, but seventy-seven times" (v. 22).

Though seventy-times-seven is an actual number, Jesus wasn't asking Peter to pull out a calculator at this moment. He was telling Peter to think even bigger—bottomless-fries bigger. He was telling Peter that there is no limit to the grace God has for us and the grace we should extend to others.

Jonah's story and Jesus' answer show us that we serve a God of more than just the second chance. We serve a God of *another* chance. He'll give us opportunity after opportunity to get this whole "walking out his will" thing right. This is because once God has made the plan, he doesn't change his mind. He never turns his back on it or on us.

I think this concept is hard for us to wrap our heads around, because it's not exactly the way the world works. When we make a big mistake in society today, often that disqualifies us from success. It's like we have one shot to achieve our dreams, and once that dream doesn't work out, we're finished for good. This is why many people who have served time in prison have trouble finding jobs after they get out. It's why politicians go to such great lengths to hide their wrongdoings. They know the minute they get exposed their careers are over. Many of us walk around in fear that our mistakes will take us out of the game.

When I played basketball in high school, my whole team played with a similar fear of our coach. He was a tall, six-foot-six-inch man with bright red hair. Sometimes I still have nightmares about his voice. No one has ever really said my name that way before or since.

If I made even one tiny mistake on the court, one wrong pass, one bad reception, if I took one bad shot, I would hear a booming, raspy, "VEACHHHHHH!" from the other side of the court. He'd be fuming with rage, the shade of his face looking more and more like the color of his hair.

Our whole team knew that the moment we made a bad move and heard that voice, someone else would be subbing for us immediately. You'd go from playing the game to warming the bench in an instant.

This created a culture of fear. My teammates and I ran around thinking, *Don't mess up. Don't make a mistake. You won't get another chance.*

Because we're used to such consequences in this life, we often expect God to work the same way. But when we mess up in our walk with him, he says, "That's all right. Get up again. We'll try for next time." He sent Jesus to save us, to shoulder the burden of our mistakes, so that we don't have to be afraid. The reason why grace came near was to remove all fear.

THE REASON WHY GRACE CAME NEAR WAS TO REMOVE ALL FEAR.

The first moment the word of the Lord came to Jonah, he rebelled, bought the wrong ticket, and found himself in a terrible storm and inside a giant fish. But this didn't disqualify him for good. As we know, the word of the Lord came a second time.

You might be asking, "How could God use me or still love me? I've smoked this. I've seen this. I've mixed with the wrong crowd. I've damaged every relationship. I've failed at the dreams

I set out to accomplish. I've done everything I shouldn't have." But God is saying, "I see the storm you've gotten yourself into. I see the fish, and I'm actually glad I have your attention now. I'm going to show you the plan again for the tenth time, the hundredth time, the seventy-times-seventh time." Because Philippians 1:6 says, "He who began a good work in you will carry it on to completion," we know that he's going to keep fighting for that same plan he initiated at the very start of our lives.

Jonah cried out in his distress. He said, "I made a mess of my life." But when he called upon God, God heard his cry. He said, "Now you're ready to walk out this plan." Verse 10 of Jonah 3 says, "When God saw what [Nineveh] did and how they turned from their evil ways, he relented and did not bring on them the destruction he had threatened."

Jonah eventually fulfilled the call. He went into the city. He told people about a loving, kind, gracious God, and revival swept across the land. He saved them from destruction and extended God's grace to them. In the end, his mistakes didn't keep him from the greatness God had planned.

DON'T DELAY YOUR DESTINY

For some of us, it can take years to finally come to that belly-of-a-whale place—the place where we say, "Okay, God. You win. I'll serve you. I'll start walking your plan out." Often we think about everything that disqualifies us. We're too flawed; we're not like the Christians we see in the limelight, on the stage, on Instagram. We've done too much, and we've gone too far. We've even run in the opposite direction. We convince ourselves of all the reasons why God should have written us off already, and it takes us years to realize that God has a plan waiting for us, no matter what.

Don't delay your destiny like Jonah did. Don't be like the Israelites, traveling to the promised land for forty years on a journey that should've taken only eleven days. It's not worth it. Why take the long way when the short way is so much . . . shorter? You don't have to wait for those tears on your pillowcase, or bumps and bruises. God will always give you another chance for greatness, but you could avoid the storm altogether. Delayed obedience is still disobedience. Learn to say yes the first time.

> **DELAYED OBEDIENCE IS STILL DISOBEDIENCE. LEARN TO SAY YES THE FIRST TIME.**

The biggest mistake I've made, and I've seen those around me do the same thing, doesn't have as much to do with making a wrong choice, but rather with delaying my obedience by doing things my own way in my own power. After I ended the relationship God was essentially forbidding, I didn't jump immediately into doing things God's way. Though outwardly I was obeying, I thought the only way to make things right was to turn to legalism.

After making that phone call, I decided I would read my Bible more, study more, be disciplined every day. My whole youth ministry was soon centered on a Bible-reading plan. This was my key to success. When people asked me, "What is the secret to your growth?" I'd answer, "Reading my Bible every day." Not that reading the Bible every day is bad; it's actually a great thing to do. But it was something I was doing out of my own strength and because I was attempting to earn God's favor. I was trying to free myself from my mistake.

But this is not the work of the believer. We often believe that God can't love us when we fail as a spouse or a leader or a parent or a follower of Jesus, so we put ourselves in jail. In doing this, we're forgetting about the gift of grace that God has given us! We're forgetting about the second chance.

The work of the believer is receiving. Today, when I make a mistake, I try to make my whole life about receiving God's grace. I work hard at that rather than at following a set of rules. This is the obedience God is asking for. Receiving means finding freedom and moving past the self-hate and destructive thinking that comes after we make mistakes. Don't let one wrong turn take you out of the game; find freedom and start walking in God's dream.

5 TAKEAWAYS

If a crippled young boy, the shame of his family, has a seat at the king's table, what do you have? If the "chief of all sinners," a murderer of innocent people, was used to spread Christianity and write our Christian theology, what could you be destined for?

I hope by now you realize that no matter your past mistakes or your present faults, God has chosen you for his perfect plan. Now, what will you do with this epiphany?

These five thoughts are for you to carry with you throughout your day:

1. Embrace grace.

Write down a list of five reasons you think God has chosen you.

Then cross out all five and write the word *grace* next to each one. God's not reviewing some résumé to see what extracurriculars you've accomplished. He's not looking over your criminal record. You are qualified because of what God's done for you, not because of anything you've done or can do.

As Ephesians 2:8 says, "It is by grace you have been

saved, through faith—and this is not from yourselves, it is the gift of God."

2. Learn to listen to God's voice.

Your own voice will often put you down and tell you that you don't measure up in some way. But it's time to learn to listen to the voice that really matters. God's voice is the one telling you about your potential. He's whispering in your ear, telling you that you have a destiny and a calling.

To grasp this, create a table with two columns. On one side put "My Thoughts" and on the other "God's Thoughts." Then under "My Thoughts," write things you struggle with when it comes to how you view yourself. Before you write God's corresponding thoughts, look to some scriptures about the way God sees you. Jeremiah 1:15 and Philippians 4:13 are great places to start. Once you have some good references from the Bible about God's view of you, go to the other side of the table and write those descriptions you've discovered that contradict your thoughts. Your chart might look something like this:

MY THOUGHTS	GOD'S THOUGHTS
Failure	Success
Forgotten	Chosen
Directionless	Called

3. Realize you're on heaven's radar.

Some of you may feel that your life has just been a series of unfortunate events. If things have gone right, you might think it was merely happenstance. This is not the way qualified people walk around. Qualified people know that God's providential hand has led them where they are today. If God "knows the plans" he has for you, and if these plans are "to give you hope and a future" (Jeremiah 29:11), then you're not a new thought to him.

4. Get some willpower.

The only way for you to walk in your destiny and this plan we've been talking about is to submit your will to God. The Bible says self-control or the ability to choose God's way over your own is a "fruit of the Spirit" (Galatians 5:22). That means it's a product or result of spending time with God. Practice taking moments out of your day, even if it's just five minutes, to quiet all the voices in your head and listen to God.

5. Remember that no one is perfect.

As you leave this section, don't forget about all the imperfections of the men and women whom God mightily used. Grab your Bible and read about them again if you need to remember. God did not use a perfect, elite set of people.

Because of this, let's not make perfection our aim. If we do, we'll fail every time. Instead, let's rest in God's love for us and allow the Holy Spirit to transform us continually. It's this transforming power that makes us qualified for the plan, not our ability to follow every rule.

If you have struggled with making mistakes or are filled with regret, be encouraged. God's not done with you yet. He's still in it for the long haul. And his goal? To transform your heart to be more like his.

Part Three

THE FAITH

How do you walk in this plan?

Chapter Six
FIRST THINGS FIRST

So far we've been throwing around big statements like "God has a plan!" and "Find God's dream for your life!" By now, I'm sure many of you are wondering exactly how someone figures out what this plan is in the first place.

Great. God has a plan. But what does that look like for me?

This is the part of the book where I lay out every single, specific step it takes to find the exact will and destiny God has assigned to you.

Okay, maybe that's an overpromise.

Because each of us has a unique journey, the means by which we figure out God's plan is sure to be just as unique. And this plan is not always simple to discover. It could take a lifetime!

No, I will not be able to give you the precise recipe for figuring out your "God Dream," but I do believe the following three steps will give you a greater understanding of your purpose.

STEP #1—DISCOVER YOUR GRACE

While I was growing up, my dad always used to say to me, "Chad, you're either going to sell a lot of cars or you're going to lead a lot of people to Jesus." (Thanks, Dad. *Super* encouraging.) At the time I had no idea what he meant.

But when I look back on that statement today, I realize that this little joke was my dad's way of helping me discover what my gift and grace was. When I was young, I had a charisma, a way of talking to people, that my dad recognized. It was this gift that God would ultimately use to grow his church.

What's your God-given grace?

I think the more you think about this question, the more you'll realize how obvious the answer is. If you're someone who has trouble self-examining, ask your friends what they think your gifts are. Don't think God is trying to hide your gifts from you. His goal is not to make this process difficult or impossible. Anyone who spends time with you regularly should be able to name a few of your strengths. And if they can't, maybe you need more attentive friends.

A person's "grace," the talents and abilities that come easier to them than they do for others, are found in all shapes and sizes.

Maybe you have a winsome personality.

Maybe you have the instincts and ability to make money.

Maybe you have administrative skills.

Maybe you have creative ideas for how to design.

Maybe you are a storyteller.

Maybe you know how to listen and instantly understand what other people are going through.

Maybe you know how to network and bring people together.

These are all gifts from God!

Whether you have an inkling of what it is you might be good at or no clue at all, it's time to discover what makes you *you*. And once the picture starts to become clear, then work on figuring out how to use whatever it is you thrive at doing for God's glory.

Paul talked about the beautiful variation of gifts that make up the church. He said:

> For by the grace given me I say to every one of you: Do not think of yourself more highly than you ought, but rather think of yourself with sober judgment, in accordance with the faith God has distributed to each of you. For just as each of us has one body with many members, and these members do not all have the same function, so in Christ we, though many, form one body, and each member belongs to all the others. We have different gifts, according to the grace given to each of us. (Romans 12:3–6)

We are all dependent on each other. For God's plan for everyone to work, he needs me to be *me*. He needs you to be you, too, however quirky that might be! He doesn't need you chasing a dream that has nothing to do with the way he made you.

I love when people at our church decide to use their specific gifts. There's one guy in our church, Nate, who is a successful lawyer. One day he approached me and asked, "Is there any way I can help the church as a lawyer? Can I volunteer my time to give you legal counsel or help you with any lawsuits or legal situations?" Another guy at our church, Chase, studied film in New York City and now lives in LA. He assembled a video crew to produce beautiful videos for our church. He uses his art to affect the people around him.

Both these guys asked, "What do I have? What can I bring?" instead of, "How can I be like that guy over there?" And because

GOD DID NOT MAKE YOU ONE WAY SO HE COULD USE YOU IN ANOTHER WAY.

of this, God has used them mightily to build our church.

God did not make you one way so he could use you in another way. He's graced you with your specific potential and talents. Discover them so you can use them to change the world.

STEP #2—GET TO THE PLACE WHERE YOU CAN GET THE MESSAGE

Among the many prophets found in the Old Testament, Jeremiah is probably my favorite. God called him out and said, "I know the plans I have for you" (Jeremiah 29:11). God used him mightily to speak to the nation of Judah.

Before the prophet really stepped into this calling, God had an interesting request for him. Jeremiah said this about his experience:

> This is the word that came to Jeremiah from the LORD: "Go down to the potter's house, and there I will give you my message." So I went down to the potter's house, and I saw him working at the wheel. But the pot he was shaping from the clay was marred in his hands; so the potter formed it into another pot, shaping it as seemed best to him. (Jeremiah 18:1–4)

God was trying to show Jeremiah in a beautiful metaphor how he would use the broken clay of his nation and form it into something beautiful. It's another great example of God's commitment to use even our ugliness and failure. But to me, the most interesting portion of Jeremiah's account in chapter 18 is God's request: "Go down to the potter's house." God could've shown Jeremiah that metaphor or told him about the marred clay right then. It wouldn't take much effort for God to whisper his plan to him while he was sitting on his couch. But that's not how God wanted to do it.

Instead, he said "Jer, I need you to get out of your comfort zone. I need you to step out of your environment. I need you to come to the potter's house. This is where you'll hear about the plan."

God was wooing Jeremiah. He was asking him to get away from it all so he could truly hear God's voice. Sometimes we don't get the word we've been hoping for or a clear understanding of the plan God has for us because we're simply not available.

We're on our phones. We've filled our calendars to the brim. We're up early to work and in bed late because of social gatherings. The busyness of life is hindering us from completely realizing the plan. Sometimes we need to step out of our regular routines in order to hear what God is saying.

As a speaker, I travel a lot, and I've found that this time away impacts my perspective. There's something uniquely helpful about getting out of your own context, your usual environment, and stepping into a different space. When I'm away, I have moments of silence. In these moments, I can listen to what God's saying. My paradigm starts to shift, and I begin to see the situation I'm in through a different lens.

No one modeled the "get away" strategy better than Jesus. Simply read his story and you'll discover it. One moment he'd be doing the nine-to-five thing, ministering with his disciples on the streets. The next, no one could find him. The disciples would go crazy, saying, "Anyone seen Jesus? You know, that guy we're always hanging with who heals lepers and stuff?" They'd try to pull out an iPhone and tap "Find My Phone." I'm sure the *Where's Waldo?* routine got old.

Jesus regularly slipped away to spend time in God's presence. He knew he needed those quiet moments with his father to figure out the plan. He knew that purpose is found in his presence.

PURPOSE IS FOUND IN HIS PRESENCE.

What do you need to do to position yourself to hear what God is saying? Where do you need to go? Maybe it's a walk. Maybe a vacation or a day spent with your phone turned off (*the horror!*). Maybe a long drive. I challenge you to put this time away from your usual routine on the calendar or set an alarm. Make it a priority to leave your comfort zone every so often. I believe God will begin revealing his specific plans for you once you go to that place. He did it for Jeremiah. He's done it for me.

STEP #3—ASK YOURSELF WHO IT'S FOR

I hate to break it to you, but this plan we've been talking about isn't about your ultimate happiness. Though joy does play a part in it, it's not about having an easy, pain-free life. It's not about whether we have achieved the world's definition of "success."

God thinks much bigger than job promotions, future spouses, and easy-go-lucky happiness. Though he cares about these things, it's time to talk about a huge portion of this plan of his . . . people.

The Harvard Grant Study is a famous psychology study done over the course of seventy-five years. Starting in 1938, 268 male graduates were studied with the hopes that the researchers could unlock the secret to living a happy and fulfilled life. Throughout the seventy-five years, Harvard researchers checked in with the men at different points in their life journey.

And what was the secret they discovered? Perhaps it may be a surprise to you, but financial success and career accolades had nothing to do with the clear majority of the subjects' happiness.[2] The results all pointed to one fact: "Connection is crucial."

George Valliant, one psychiatrist who worked on the study, said, "Joy is connection. The more areas in your life you can make connection, the better. . . . The conclusion of the study, not in a medical but in a psychological sense, is that connection is the whole shooting match." Those in this study with the strongest relational ties, even if they had career failures or a lack of societal success, ended up being the happiest. God made us for connection.

Our purpose will always be tied to people. Examine your own dream, and ask yourself, "If I achieve this, who will it be for?" If the answer is yourself, that dream will most likely end up shattered. Or you may achieve it and find it was worth nothing. Regardless, if you think you know the plan God has for you and it has nothing to do with his people, you're probably on the wrong track. Philippians 2:13 says, "For it is God who works in you, both to will and to work for his good pleasure" (ESV). What is this good pleasure? The people he's created and loves.

It's all about others.

Isn't it interesting that when the word of the Lord came to Jonah, when Jesus overflowed Peter's ship and called him forward, when Paul's eyes were blinded on the road, it wasn't only for Jonah, Peter, and Paul to feel good about themselves? The promises they received were all about the people they would reach, the lives they would touch, and the nations they would save. It was about how God would use them to affect the lives of others.

I believe that God has plans for every person's life. You should be blown away at how great and wonderful these plans are. They're not the ordinary plans we conjure up in our tiny human brains. His plans are not to make you famous, rich, known, or powerful, because he's looking to do something so much larger than yourself.

WHO COULD YOUR "NO" AFFECT?

It's not just our lives on the line here. When Jonah said, "No!" initially, he nearly kept salvation from an entire people group! Who could your "no" affect?

Chapter Seven
ASKING FOR A FRIEND

When it comes to asking for favors or hookups, what kind of person are you? Are you the type who walks around with over-the-top confidence? Do you have no social radar and no fear of humiliation? Do you have no problem asking people for things?

I call these people the big askers. They don't have any hesitation when it comes to hitting up their friends for just about everything. They typically feel they have nothing to lose in the relationship, so they decide to take the chance and call in a favor when they need it.

I lean more on the shy side. I'd rather not ruffle the feathers of those around me. I'd rather not risk offending someone or embarrassing myself. I've always felt like this. But in the last few years, as I've found myself in LA and hanging out with more and more people who are in the limelight and influential, it's gotten worse. Because I know these friends are constantly being hit up for swag, I tend to err on the side of caution even more. I would never want someone to think I have ulterior motives or only want to use them to gain something.

I'm what you might call a non-asker, but only when it comes to myself. If it's something that I need or want, I refuse to phone a friend. I'll figure out how to get it on my own. But, oddly, this personal rule of mine doesn't apply when someone else is in need. Just a few weeks ago some friends wanted tickets to a basketball game, and I happened to know someone who had great season tickets. Season tickets that, even though I had known this person for quite a while, I had never asked to use for myself. But because I was asking for a friend, I felt okay about the whole thing, and I texted for the tickets.

This same odd practice applies to parties too. If I'm getting ready for an event and I'm not sure what the dress code is, I never ask the person throwing the party what I should wear. This definitely would be against my principles. I typically just do my very best guesswork. I'll throw on some nice jeans. I might even poke some holes in them if need be. I come prepared with scissors or a jacket to adapt my outfit if necessary. Anything is better than asking for yourself, even if it means having to get arts and crafty with your outfit at a party.

But if someone else asks me what they should wear for the night, I won't think twice about grabbing my phone, texting the host, and saying, "Yo, I'm good. Yeah, I'm cool, but Chuck on the other hand . . . Well, he wants to know what he's supposed to wear to this thing."

It's all cool if Chuck's the one asking.

Because of this worldview, I find myself shocked when someone breaks my little code of conduct and brazenly asks for something for themselves. When people slip a Big Ask casually into a conversation, I usually feel betrayed. I've had some people start off text threads all friendly. They throw a "How you been?" at me and follow with a couple of emojis and an "lol" or two.

Then, all of a sudden . . . BAM! They hit me with a question and finally get to what they really wanted all along.

I haven't been able to get ahold of the yeezies . . .

Do you think you could hook me up?

I was really hoping you could introduce me to so-and-so.

Could you make that happen?

A text like that elicits an "Oh, no, you didn't!" and never gets a response from me. For some reason I believe that asking for a friend is socially allowed while asking for yourself is completely unacceptable. And I know I'm not the only one who thinks this way.

The funny thing about this unspoken rule and expectation is that it leaks into a lot of our perspectives on God. In my own life, I've noticed that I often have no problem asking God to do something for other people. I'll pray for a friend's finances, relationships, and health.

"Hey, God, would you give Mary a raise?"

"God, heal Cole's cancer!"

"God, open up the door for new job opportunities for Daniel."

Asking for another's healing, career, or future is acceptable and easy, but I often struggle going to God and asking him to do big things for me. This is in part due to my broken dreams. For instance, in 2008, I decided to come before God with a bold ask and then saw my dreams get crushed. I would later realize it was just a small delay before a huge victory, but at the time it rattled me. It scared me away from asking for quite a long time. But asking is such a crucial part of walking out the plans God has for us.

Once you've discovered your plan or have a better

understanding of what God has called you to, you may be wondering what it looks like to be pursuing it, to be doing God's will on a daily basis. It starts by getting over our weird rules and making the Big Ask. Perhaps the reason many aren't walking into God's perfect potential for their lives is because they don't know how to ask for themselves.

If the Bible says, "You do not have because you do not ask" (James 4:2), and if Jesus himself said, "Ask and it will be given to you; seek and you will find; knock and the door will be opened" (Matthew 7:7), it's clear that asking plays a huge part in this faith thing. If you're going to be a faith person, you can't talk to God shyly like you're texting a friend on behalf of a friend who's wondering what to wear to a party that night. If you're going to be a faith person, you have to learn to confidently make the Big Ask.

And what is this Big Ask? It could look a little something like this:

"God, use me and help me walk in my full potential."

"God, open this door for me."

"God, give me the future that you designed."

I like how Hebrews 11:6 lays out faith as the prerequisite for coming to God. It says, "Without faith it is impossible to please God, because anyone who comes to him must believe that he exists and that he rewards those who earnestly seek him."

To confidently make the Big Ask, you have to come to God with an understanding that he actually cares about you. You need to believe that he genuinely listens to your cries and is ready to help you in whatever situation you may face. He's not like our fickle human friends, whom we worry may reject us and not text back after we make the Big Ask. He is ready and standing by, eagerly waiting for us to ask for these things so that he can reward us as his sons and daughters! But you need an under-standing of who he is. You'll never make the Big Ask until you believe that he's a big God.

IT'S NOT ENOUGH TO JUST ASK

If you comb through the Bible, you'll find some pretty big askers, and you'll typically find Jesus commending these individuals for their asking. But sometimes you find people who ask and don't receive.

What separates the ones who ask and receive from the askers who don't? The answer is faith. One of my personal favorite stories of an Ask Gone Wrong shows up in Matthew 17. It's the story of a desperate father with a child in need of a miracle.

> **YOU'LL NEVER MAKE THE BIG ASK UNTIL YOU BELIEVE THAT HE'S A BIG GOD.**

This father watched his son going through something no parent ever wants their child to go through. His kid was being tossed into the fire and thrown into the ocean because of demons! That's something you wouldn't wish on your worst enemy, let alone your own little boy. We all dream of a child in perfect health. I myself know what it feels like when a dream like this is crushed.

Because of his awful circumstance, the father decided to turn to the church for help. I'm sure he thought, *A disciple of Jesus should do the trick! The church will know what to do with my son. Jesus has been healing people left and right; I'm sure his followers can handle this.*

And so he found nine disciples, standing by, ready to help the poor kid. But after the disciples tried to heal his son, nothing happened. His son remained tortured by these demons, and the father was forced to leave without his request answered. His Big Ask had failed.

It was on his way back from this failed attempt that the father encountered Jesus. Jesus had been away from the group with his three compadres, Peter, James, and John. They had just been on top of a mountain, where the crazy transfiguration had taken place. If you don't know that story, it's definitely one of the more trippy ones in the Bible. They had just been hanging out with Moses and Elijah (both dead at the time, by the way), and the first thing they encountered on their return home was this dad with a broken dream and a sick child.

When the father saw Jesus, he instantly fell to his knees and prepared to make the Big Ask. Verses 15–16 pick up the story: "'Lord, have mercy on my son,' he said. 'He has seizures and is suffering greatly. He often falls into the fire or into the water. I brought him to your disciples, but they could not heal him.'"

Jesus listened to the man's request, but before he addressed him and his son's needs, he turned to the crowd that was there. Because Jesus was teaching and ministering in Galilee, he knew the usual suspects would be present. Galilee was a little bit like the bar from *Cheers*, and Jesus knew all their names. There were scholars, Bible teachers, religious people, scribes, and tax collectors. This was where they always hung out. And they were all watching to see what Jesus would do about this demon-possessed boy and Jesus' followers who had failed to heal him.

Instead of looking at the dad, who was on his knees, Jesus decided instead to speak to the usual suspects. "My God! How long do I have to put up with you all?!" he yelled. "I've been here . . . what . . . thirty-three years? Beam me up, Scotty! I'm out!"

Okay, so these weren't his exact words, but they do sum up Jesus' level of frustration at that moment in time.

Jesus was dealing with a generation of skeptics. In the Old Testament, long before Jesus had walked the earth, the Bible foretold this generation. The Old Testament had predicted that they would be a group of faithless people, always watching God's work with one eyebrow raised. And it all came to pass.

Because of this, Jesus addressed the crowd before talking to the man and his son. He knew why this father's ask had failed. He turned to the crowd and said, "You unbelieving and perverse generation . . . How long shall I stay with you? How long shall I put up with you?" (v. 17).

You see, the reason the boy didn't get healed by the nine disciples was not because God couldn't heal the boy or didn't want to cast out the demons. It wasn't because God's plan for that boy was to live a life of torment. The reason the boy didn't get healed was because there was no faith in that town. Perhaps the disciples had a little faith, but the skeptics around them were crossing their arms and looking on. The faithless were watching and waiting for Jesus and his followers to mess up, saying, "Let's see what you can do, huh? Let's see if you can actually heal this kid." And I'm sure this skepticism affected the disciples' belief in what was possible. Just as we often crack under the pressure of the skepticism of others, the disciples, too, had a hard time believing in the positive possibility when surrounded by negative scoffers.

Because of their lack of belief, the boy continued to suffer.

In Mark's account of the story, Jesus brought the boy out in front of the crowd and allowed the demon to show himself to all who were watching.

Mark 9:26–27 says, "The spirit shrieked, convulsed him violently and came out. The boy looked so much like a corpse that many said, 'He's dead.' But Jesus took him by the hand and lifted him to his feet, and he stood up."

Jesus ultimately delivered the boy. But he also demonstrated that we can't do anything in our own power. We must have faith in the one greater than us. The disciples were in the right place at the right time. Jesus had already given them authority to heal and cast out demons. They thought they would be successful and were baffled when they failed.

In their bafflement, the disciples pulled Jesus aside. "Help us out here. Why in the world could we not heal this kid?" they asked. They thought they had done everything right. They had healed people in the past. What went wrong this time?

Jesus answered this way in Matthew 17:20: "Because you have so little faith." Faith is the key to walking in your potential. If the disciples were to perform miracles on Jesus' behalf, they had to have faith. To walk in God's plan, they couldn't crack under the pressure of their environment. They had to stand strong and believe.

Don't worry. Jesus didn't leave them there. He continued with this thought: "Truly I tell you, if you have faith as small as a mustard seed, you can say to this mountain, 'Move from here to there,' and it will move. Nothing will be impossible for you" (v. 20).

MOVING MOUNTAINS STARTS WITH TRUSTING GOD TODAY.

First, you have to be willing to make the Big Ask; but second, you have to have faith when you make that ask. Jesus is telling his disciples that then, and only then, will that mountain, that obstacle that's in your way, that addiction you're facing, that relationship that's holding you back, or that sickness that's breaking you move out of your way. Then and only then will you walk out his plan. Moving mountains starts with trusting God today.

WHEN THE ANSWER DISAPPOINTS

It was 2008. I was standing behind the stage, sweating. This was it, the conference I had put all my hopes and dreams in. I had prayed over and over again for it to be a huge success. I was even audacious enough to ask God for specific numbers.

My girlfriend at the time, Julia, would be there. This was the first time I'd be showing her what I did for work. This would be the big moment where she would see that I was a great youth leader. She would realize all the lives I was impacting in Seattle.

The worship music was booming. I heard kids screaming. It sounded like it could be a big crowd. But was it? Would kids get saved? Would anyone care? Would the image I saw of myself in the future finally be fulfilled? Would I be good enough?

I walked onto the stage before the song was over. I knew it was time to get the event going. My time for questions was over. I made my way out.

And then my heart instantly sank and dropped into my shoes. Hundreds of eyes stared back at me, but I could only see one thing.

The chairs were only half full!

I didn't pay attention to all the kids who were there, ready to worship, excited to hear from God. All I saw were the cold, dusty seats. The entire room might as well have been empty. A resounding echo, displaying my failure as a leader.

I looked at Julia's encouraging face. I tried to shake off my disappointment and looked at the audience.

The numbers I had asked God for, the dream I had hoped for, all of it had failed.

I'll never ask like that again, I thought.

Have you ever asked God for something, believed he would grant your request with all your heart, and still found yourself disappointed in the answer, or what seemed like a lack of answer? Sometimes it's because of a lack of faith, like we saw in the story of the demon-possessed boy, but sometimes it's because we don't have God's perspective. Sometimes what would be best for us is a "no" from God. Other times it might be a "not yet" because we're not quite ready for a full "yes" and need to learn and grow before its complete realization. It's hard to see what's going on while we're in it, though, and it can be disheartening. So disheartening, at times, that we resolve not to ask anymore, like I did after that conference. But this is not the best way to go. We may not understand God's answer of "no" or "wait," but we shouldn't allow that to turn us into non-askers.

WHY WE CAN ASK

Why are we able to ask an all-powerful, all-knowing, all-seeing God for help? Why can we ask for a better life and future with him? There's really only one reason. This reason is the object of our faith. Because of this object, we can boldly come to God with our needs and wants and receive answers. It is not faith in and of itself. We don't put stock in the fact that we know how to believe. It's the object of our faith: Jesus. It's in him that we put our faith. It's not in our amazing confession or how good we are at asking or believing. It's all about him. It's because of who he is that we can continue asking, even when we've heard "no" or "wait" in the past.

Walking into God's plan and truly living by faith come by understanding that Jesus is the source of our faith. "By grace you have been saved, through faith—and this is not from yourselves, it is the gift of God" (Ephesians 2:8).

This grace that has saved us is not some principle. Grace is a person. It's Jesus. And it's not ourselves and our amazing faith that transform our lives; it's this grace from Jesus. All our confidence and all our faith have to be wrapped up in the Son. Because of him, we can approach God, ask with boldness, and see mountains move. Because of him, we don't have to beat ourselves up for that relationship we let go on too long or that job opportunity that fizzled. Because of him, we can dream differently and see those God-ordained dreams come to fruition.

Let's say you're going to a horse race and have to pick a horse to win. Maybe you choose Clever Donkey. (Not sure why a horse would be called Clever Donkey, but just go with it.) You arrive and give the guy at the booth your money. "I'm going to put all my money on Clever Donkey!" you say. "Clever Donkey will win this race!"

Then you watch the race. And Clever Donkey starts coming around the track. In that moment, your whole body is filled with confidence and hope in Clever Donkey. Because you put your money on the line, you expect that horse to win this race.

It's also a little bit like when you watch Steph Curry as he's about to shoot a three-pointer on TV. You'll see an entire arena holding their breaths, waiting for him to make it. Everybody stands and watches the ball as he shoots it. They wait eagerly as it makes its famous high arc. And if he misses, the whole room gasps in shock. If Steph Curry doesn't make his three-pointer, the room cannot believe it. Why? Because we've put our hope and confidence in his abilities as a shooter.

Luckily, unlike a horse or an NBA player, Jesus always wins. If you put your faith, your money, your life, and all your confidence and hope in him, he won't let you down. It's because of him that you can even ask God in the first place. Through his death and resurrection, he bore our sins and made a way for us to go straight to God. Because of him, we have an incredible future in front of us.

It bothers me when Christians make faith about something that it's not. I hate seeing faith become some kind of accent or personality. I'm not a huge fan of the strange subculture that defines itself as the ones "walking in faith" yet is really just putting all their faith in themselves. Faith is not about your own doing. It's about the gift of Jesus. We'll talk more about this Jesus, the central part of God's plan, later. For now, understand that it's faith in him that opens up the door of possibility. Faith in him leads to lives saved and bodies healed.

> **DOUBT AND THE DEVIL SAY, "WAIT FOR TOMORROW." FAITH AND THE FATHER SAY, "ASK TODAY."**

The father in Matthew 17 knew the disciples weren't the source. When things didn't work out at the church, he went straight to Jesus to ask for help. It's time for us all to go straight to the source with complete confidence that he can move any mountain and help us walk into our future. Let's go straight to Jesus and make the Big Ask.

What are you asking God for? Don't wait to get to heaven

one day and wish that you would've believed for more. Don't arrive at eternity and wish you would've asked for more in this life. Doubt and the Devil say, "Wait for tomorrow." Faith and the Father say, "Ask today."

Now is the time to start asking for God's plan! Yes, maybe you'll see failure like I did at the conference years ago. But you might realize later that you were asking for all the wrong reasons and God had a better plan anyway. Ask with God on your side, and you'll see what it's like to walk in his better dream.

Chapter Eight
STEP OUT

I don't know if you're the type of person who still has cable TV. We seem to be a dying breed these days. I personally need my cable and my DVR. I'm what you might call "a DVRer-er." Every day at 3:00 p.m. I record *Pardon the Interruption*, my favorite sports program. I also DVR the Grammys, the Oscars, sports games. If it's live, only on once, and I'm not around, I will DVR it.

That's right. I'm the guy who DVRs that important game and shows up at the party, praying that nobody tells me the score. I'm not a fan of the other guy at the party who loves spoiling things.

"Oh, you DVR'd the game?! Really? Do you want to know the score?"

This sort of prodding by Spoiler Guy will always get a cold stare from me, followed by "No. I'm good. Thanks."

"You sure you don't wanna know?"

The reason Spoiler Guy and all the other spoilers out there ask again is because they can't help themselves. Even when they're trying to be good about not ruining last night's episode or game, they hint at the ending. They make some sort of sly, hidden statement in passing that lets you know what's going on.

"I won't tell you what happens, but . . . you're going to be surprised. That's all I'll say!"

This sort of hint is exactly what I do *not* want.

Most of you are probably like me and find spoilers very frustrating. You don't want to invest in a movie, TV show, or game if you know exactly what's going to happen in the end.

This is probably why I have such a beef with going to the movie theater these days. Don't get me wrong, I love seeing movies. I'll take my wife, my boo thing, my squeeze, and we'll pay the $200 to get in. We'll get the popcorn, the soda, the Milk Duds, the Twizzlers, and the peanut M&M's.

That's how we do it at the movies.

But the overpriced snacks are not my problem with the whole event. My main issue is with the previews. When you watch the trailer of a movie, you are basically watching the whole entire movie. In three minutes, you'll meet every character and learn every plot point. You'll discover who lives, who dies, who gets married, and who gets divorced. I usually think to myself, *Why would I even go see this movie now?*

Spoilers are the worst, but teasers I can get behind. The difference between a teaser and a preview is that a teaser only gives you a glimpse of the movie you'll see one day. It whets your appetite with a couple of seconds of an epic battle scene or a close-up of your favorite actor. It gets you pumped with an exciting score and one or two cryptic words of dialogue. It promises a great story without telling you exactly how this great story plays out.

God is just like that. I love that he's a teaser, not a spoiler. He never tells you all that your tomorrow holds but gives you glimpses and promises of your future along the way. This is because God won't show you what he has for you tomorrow until you're faithful with what he's given you today.

Most of us chase after the previews of life. We want to know everything that's going to happen to us. We chase the five-year plans or the "how to be successful" semi-nars, because they lay out the dream for us in very simple and tangible steps. They give us an exact image of the money and fame that we'll achieve.

I hate to break it to you, but life isn't always that simple and easy. God's plan may not be as tangible as the one you tried and failed at achieving.

How do we walk through this today without knowing how it will all play out? How do we walk out God's plan if we don't know the entire story? Most of us want God

> **GOD WON'T SHOW YOU WHAT HE HAS FOR YOU TOMORROW UNTIL YOU'RE FAITHFUL WITH WHAT HE'S GIVEN YOU TODAY.**

to give us the preview version. We want to know the ending—who dies, who lives, how things go down. But living out God's dream starts with trusting.

"Those who know your name trust in you, for you, LORD, have never forsaken those who seek you" (Psalm 9:10). If we know the character of God, we can trust that he will finish what he's started.

THE TRUST FALL

Think of your life with God like one giant trust fall.

In a trust fall, you close your eyes, fold your arms over your chest, and allow yourself to fall into the arms of those around you without flinching or worrying. It's all about feeling confident that your friends, classmates, or coworkers will catch you, and it goes against everything your natural instincts tell you to do. While you free-fall backward into the unknown, your head is telling you to turn around and take a peek in order to ensure your partner really does have his or her arms stretched out for you. Your muscles are telling you to reach out and catch yourself. These natural instincts are good. Your body doesn't want you to plummet to the ground and get injured. But to have a successful trust fall, you have to let go and take that first step of trust.

Trust is a funny thing. Just as in this weird exercise, at some point in your relationship with each person around you, you have to take that first step of trust. When you initiate a new friendship, you're trusting that the person will treat you well, not slander your name to others, and be there for you when you need them. When you take a recommendation for a new Mediterranean restaurant or watch a movie's teaser and then decide to eat at that restaurant or see that movie, your actions demonstrate your trust in a person's taste or a trailer's promise. You must choose to take that first step.

You can also choose to stop trusting those around you. Maybe a friend started some rumor. Maybe a remark was spoken that hurt your feelings. Just as we can take a step toward trusting someone, we can also take a step away from trusting someone.

If you closely examine your life, you might be surprised to discover that many of your decisions are based on this thing called trust. Trust is a big deal, and if you want to live out the great plan that God has for your life and move past the destruction that came with your broken dream, it's a necessary step.

Proverbs 3:5–6 talks about the importance of a life motivated by trust, saying, "Trust in the LORD with all your heart and lean not on your own understanding; in all your ways submit to him, and he will make your paths straight."

To drop everything and submit to God every step of the way, you first have to be completely confident in who he is. He is all-knowing, all-powerful, and all about you. He's ready to walk with you through his plan because he loves you unconditionally. You can expect him to get you to your best possible tomorrow, but you can't expect him to lay it all out for you. Remember, it's not a three-minute movie trailer that spoils your entire story. You have to trust that he will get you there one day at a time.

WITH EVERYDAY FAITH, WE ACCESS GOD'S PLAN. TRUST IS SAYING, "HE CAN."

This is the key to experiencing your best possible tomorrow. Having the faith to trust God each day is the means by which you can access his plan. It's not by your own accomplishments, talents, or strengths that you walk into an amazing future. Most of you have realized this after failing time and time again. It's all about trusting Jesus, the object of our faith. With everyday faith, we access God's plan. Trust is saying, "He can."

STEP OUT OF THE BOAT

Let's look at Peter's life again. Peter was one trusting guy, and he displayed his trust in Jesus with his outward actions.

Multiple times throughout his story, Peter took a step that demonstrated his internal faith. Three times, specifically, the fisherman stepped out of the boat he was in and revealed his confidence that Jesus had a better plan for him.

The first time Peter took a step out of the boat was after Jesus preached the sermon on the lake and overflowed Peter's boat with fish. Though he had no idea who Jesus was at that time, he trusted that he was holy and worth abandoning everything for. He and the other fishermen "left everything and followed him" (Luke 5:11). This was the ultimate trust fall. Only, rather than risking a little bruise or a coworker accidentally dropping them, the disciples were risking their entire means of earning a living!

They dropped their nets, left their boats, and ditched all their belongings. Something about the person of Jesus filled them with instant trust. Because of that trust, they stepped out of the boat.

The second time Peter took a step of faith like this is recorded in Matthew 14. This time, instead of overflowing the boats with fish, Jesus displayed superhuman powers and walked on top of water. I think we've heard the phrase "walking on water" so much as a culture that the reality of the situation doesn't quite hit us. But the disciples had never seen a superhero movie. There were no such things as special effects in Galilee. I'm sure the sight of a man walking where he should've been sinking was shocking. The disciples were probably looking around at each other, jaws dropped, wondering what exactly was going on.

But not Peter. Peter saw this man whom he'd now come to love doing the miraculous again. And he was so focused on him that he was filled with trust and confidence. He saw him and instantly had the kind of faith that says, "I can experience something this epic and unimaginable too!"

Peter said, "Lord, if it's you . . . tell me to come to you on the water" (Matthew 14:28). And Jesus replied, "Come" (v. 29). And so again, filled with this assurance that Jesus would take care of him, Peter got out of the boat and took a step of faith. And he experienced the miraculous just like Jesus!

Until . . .

. . . he stopped experiencing the miraculous.

For Peter, the story took a bit of an unfortunate turn right about here. The story continues with, "But when he saw the wind, he was afraid and, beginning to sink, cried out, 'Lord, save me!'" (v. 30).

Peter started to lose trust. He peeked behind his back during the most important trust fall. Maybe he remembered the times in his past when things didn't go according to plan. Perhaps his past thwarted his belief. Or maybe he was just scared of the unknown. Whatever the reason, he questioned whether Jesus was really going to catch him. And he sank. He sank hard.

This second step of trust Peter took was a bit of a failure in the end, but thankfully Jesus decided to turn this embarrassing sinking disaster into a teaching moment. "You of little faith!" he said, revealing that faith is something that can be measured and something that we can all grow in. "Why did you doubt?" (v. 31).

Fortunately, as we know, Peter's story did not end there. Because God truly is "the same yesterday and today and forever" (Hebrews 13:8), he didn't abandon his plan for Peter's life because of Peter's failures. Peter was given a third chance to step out of a boat. He had made a mistake. But just as God did in Jonah's story, he gave Peter another chance to walk out the plan, to step out of the boat, and to live a life of faith.

This next incident did not come about just because of Jesus' holiness or only as a result of a display of his power. Peter took a step of faith because of Jesus' love. When Jesus arrived at the Sea of Galilee after his death and resurrection, Peter jumped out of his boat again (John 21). Despite that he had denied Jesus three times earlier that week, Jesus still showed up on the shore. He still took the time to meet with Peter and call him to a greater life.

Peter jumped out of the boat this third time because of the compassion he'd seen Jesus display for all. Because he had walked with Jesus and still experienced love despite all his failings, Peter put his whole trust in him. Jesus was indeed the object of Peter's faith.

John 21 says:

> Then the disciple whom Jesus loved said to Peter, "It is the Lord!" As soon as Simon Peter heard him say, "It is the Lord," he wrapped his outer garment around him (for he had taken it off) and jumped into the water. The other disciples followed in the boat, towing the net full of fish, for they were not far from shore, about a hundred yards. (vv. 7–8)

WE SHOULD BE MOVING PAST STATUS QUO AND RUNNING TOWARD JESUS SO WE CAN GROW.

This is what taking a step of faith in response to God's grace looks like. Like Peter, we should be plunging out of the water and running toward the one who loves us and has a plan for our lives. We should be moving past status quo and running toward Jesus so we can grow.

Like it did for Peter, this all starts with faith.

WHAT EXACTLY IS FAITH ANYWAY?

- "The righteous will live by faith" (Romans 1:17).
- "Without faith it is impossible to please God, because anyone who comes to him must believe that he exists and that he rewards those who earnestly seek him" (Hebrews 11:6).
- "Then [Jesus] touched their eyes and said, 'According to your faith, let it be done to you'" (Matthew 9:29).
- "'Go,' said Jesus, 'your faith has healed you'" (Mark 10:52).

If you read pretty much any section of the Bible, you'll quickly discover that faith is a big deal. If it's "impossible to please God," as Hebrews says, without an understanding of who he is and a belief in who he is, then we should probably figure out how to understand and believe. We should probably learn exactly what it is God is asking of us.

My favorite definition of faith is in Hebrews 11, where the author walks us through the ultimate Faith Hall of Fame. He tells us how all the heroes of the Bible lived by this life-changing action. But he starts these stories with a clean statement that sums up what this faith thing is all about.

"Now faith," he says, "is confidence in what we hope for and assurance about what we do not see" (v. 1). This means that faith has both a future element and an invisible element. God promises us an amazing future, and if we have confidence in this future, we have faith. But this future and perfect plan can't be seen, and that's where belief and the trust fall come into play. Because we do not know what our best possible tomorrows look like and we have not seen God in the flesh, we have to trust and believe. We have to walk around with this belief and let this faith affect every part of our lives. This is how we walk in the plan.

Paul put it this way: "In him we live and move and have our being" (Acts 17:28). If we have faith and are walking out God's plan, we're living and moving and having our being in something we can't see. It's not tangible. It's not something we can reach out and touch. But when we choose to put our faith in God's presence and Spirit, we see the rewards of "those who earnestly seek him" that Hebrews 11:6 talks about.

> **A LOT OF PEOPLE WANT THE REWARDS OF GOD BUT DON'T WANT TO TAKE STEPS TOWARD GOD.**

And what are these "rewards"? The realization of the big plan God has for your life! The joy of walking in your God-given potential! The ability to move past yesterday's heartaches and low points into our best possible tomorrow! This is what comes when we take the step of faith and earnestly seek after God. A lot of people want the rewards of God but don't want to take steps toward God. Let's start taking some steps.

BABY STEPS TO CALIFORNIA

I'm imagining that you, the reader, are starting to unfollow me right about now. "Oh, so now you're telling me I need to walk around with an invisible spirit inside of me and everything will just work out, Chad? Should I also stop showering and dance around in flower crowns like some girl at Coachella?"

The reality is that this faith thing doesn't have to be weird.

Throughout my life, I've had to take steps of faith just like Peter did. I've had to trust in someone I couldn't see, in the person of Jesus. Sometimes these steps came in the form of small, everyday decisions. Should I reach out to this person? Should I answer this phone call? Should I put my money in this place?

Other times the decisions have been larger and more life-altering. One of my first large faith steps came when I decided to move to LA for the first time to go to Bible college. My original plan was to attend Central Washington University like my parents had. I would become a basketball coach and a teacher. I was sure about what my future looked like.

But then God started moving me toward a different plan for my life. Suddenly I couldn't get Bible college out of my mind. I could feel God calling me to give up the Central Washington University dream and move to LA. So, I decided to take that blind step of faith. I wish I could tell you that I threw my whole heart and soul into Bible college and the big move to LA. I wish I could tell you that I was like Peter, plunging into the water from the boat, ready to do exactly what God had called me to do. But my big step of faith was a little bit more of a baby step.

"I'll go for one year," I told God. "And then I'll come back up to Central Washington." At least that would be a step. That would have to count for something, right? Sometimes only one step toward God's plan is all it takes to open up many doors.

My freshman year of college went by, and it was great. But I still had my plan and my original deal with God. I would get through that year and then head back up to Ellensberg, Washington, to be a Wildcat and make Dad proud.

The last day of the semester came, and I was saying good-bye to all the friends I had made, hugging necks, exchanging telephone numbers, telling everybody that was it for me. But then I got another sense that my dream was not the right dream.

I felt God telling me I wasn't supposed to go back north. He had more for me in southern California. My faith and trust began to build, and I got excited about this invisible future God seemed to be calling me to. And so I stayed in LA and finished Bible college.

Faith is not always easy. Trusting in a God you can't physically see and having confidence in the stories you read in the Bible and the testimony of others can be difficult. But let me tell you from my own experience that there is something that exceeds expectations on the other side of stepping out.

I don't even like to think of what my life would look like if I had returned and gone to my father's alma mater. If I hadn't followed God's leading and trusted that Bible college was the right place for me, and specifically a Bible college in LA, I wouldn't be standing where I am today. While I was in LA, I began to fall in love with the city and the people. Though I ended up eventually moving north to pastor in Seattle, I couldn't shake the city from my heart. And so, in 2014, I moved back to start Zoe LA with my family.

Looking back on this story only makes me more excited about my future. When I reflect on the moments I've chosen to take steps of faith and see now where those steps have taken me, I get excited about continuing to trust God more every day.

WE'RE CONVINCED

Even though we experience times when we clearly see the fruit of trusting God, sometimes it's still difficult to choose faith in the middle of our everyday moments. This is something Jesus' followers struggled with even while he was still with them. In fact, some of his followers deserted him in the middle of his ministry! It's hard to imagine losing trust in a man who walks on water, heals the sick, and performs miracle after miracle. But it was Jesus' teaching that turned some of them away.

In John 6:35, Jesus preached to his disciples about being the "bread of life." We're used to hearing this phrase these days, but try to put yourself in the followers' shoes. Jesus was telling them, "Whoever eats my flesh and drinks my blood has eternal life" (v. 54).

It was upon hearing this *Twilight*-level weird stuff that "many of his disciples turned back and no longer followed him" (v. 66). True, Jesus' words were strange and mysterious. They had that invisible quality like so many of God's requests for our lives have. But if those disciples had stuck around a little while longer, they would've seen the grand plan in it all. They would've realized that Jesus wasn't trying to be Edward Cullen. Jesus was talking in metaphor and pointing to the sacrifice he would one day make on the cross.

My favorite part of this story is what comes next. After these haters abandoned Jesus, he turned to the Twelve and asked, "You do not want to leave too, do you?" (v. 67).

This is where good old faithful Peter stepped up again and said, "Lord, to whom shall we go? You have the words of eternal life. We have come to believe and to know that you are the Holy One of God" (vv. 68–69). This is a beautiful example of faith.

With this statement, Peter was saying that he and the other disciples were convinced. They had left their homes and their businesses, abandoned their farms, all to follow Jesus! They wouldn't have done that if they weren't absolutely certain that he, and he alone, was the key to it all.

Peter was ready to walk out the whole plan, vampire-talk and all. He was ready to see where God would lead him, even if he didn't have a complete understanding of the whole picture.

Unless you're convinced like Peter was that Jesus is holy, true, and the key to eternal life, you're not going to sell the farm and abandon everything. Unless you are sure that he's real and what the Bible says about him holds up, you're not going to give up that business or grand idea for God's plan. Unless you know beyond a shadow of a doubt that God is real and has a future for you, you'll continue to watch your dreams crumble around you. Disappointment could become your everyday reality unless you finally decide to trust, to believe, to choose the best possible tomorrow God had planned all along.

YOU'LL ALWAYS LIVE WITH A BROKEN DREAM UNTIL YOU EXCHANGE IT FOR GOD'S BETTER DREAM.

Once you take the first step out of the boat, leave your plan behind to fully trust in God, and begin the journey of discovering his plan fully, you don't look back. Romans 4:21 defines faith as "being fully persuaded that God [has] the power to do what he had promised." It's time for us all to get fully persuaded and convinced of God's promises and plan. You'll always live with a broken dream until you exchange it for God's better dream. But your first action has to be faith.

Chapter Nine
YOU MOVE, I MOVE

I've always been a mover. I'm not the type of person who is content just lying around all day, Netflixing. Something inside of me is always pulling me to get out, get active, and move around. This can be problematic on vacations or holidays, when everyone settles in with a good book or a TV series for hours and hours.

Me? I'm usually planning my exit. Sure, I can watch a movie. But once that movie is over, I'm ready for the next big thing. I'm ready to get out and do something.

I'll blame this on my elementary school self. As I've mentioned, I grew up playing basketball. A lot of basketball. My elementary, middle, and high school coaches all had the same offense strategy. They called it "Motion Offense." Basically, the goal was to never stop moving and to always be intentionally doing some sort of action on the court. If you were simply standing and waiting for something to happen, you weren't playing the game.

Somehow Motion Offense and this rule of constant movement have stuck with me through adulthood. Today, the first thing I think when I wake up in the morning is, *Let's do this!*

And I go, go, go, to meetings, to exercise, to hangouts, laughing, building, sharing, moving . . . until it's time for bed.

Because of this little quirk, I absolutely loathe those moments when I find myself stuck in a place or situation. A Motion Offensive player cannot get stuck. What would my former coaches think?

Recently my wife and I and our three kids all found ourselves in an elevator. We all know how an elevator works. Its job is to move you from one location to another. You might be going up; you might be going down. But if you're in an elevator, you're probably moving. Unless, of course, you're in the elevator we were in on this particular day. The five of us stepped into the usually trusty machine, pushed that reliable button, watched as the doors closed us in, and then . . . nothing happened. We were stuck.

In that terrifying moment, as my kids were screaming and my wife was stressing, I should've stepped up as the man. I, with my four manly chest hairs, should've owned the whole situation. I should've, but I didn't.

Instead, I looked at my wife and said, "I just want you to know I'm about to have a panic attack. You're going to have to take care of me too." I committed to this promise, having a panic attack for the whole forty-five minutes it took for us to get out of there. (Okay, so it was more like five minutes. But it felt like four hours, so I split the difference when I tell the story.)

I'm not a huge fan of being unable to move. I'm the guy who walks into the party and scans the room for the talkers, the ones who trap you into two-hour-long conversations. I will avoid this personality type like the plague.

I'm also the guy who always has to live at least two turns

from the freeway for fear of being stuck in traffic or at a red light for an extended period of time. One of my friends, the poor soul, lives all the way out in West Hollywood and miles from any of LA's one thousand freeways. I usually tell him we should hang at my house. (I mean, I don't want to have *another* panic attack, right?)

As crazy as my Motion Offense strategy may sound when applied to everyday life, I think God has a similar strategy. If you look closely at the Bible and his story, you'll quickly learn that God is a god of movement. You never find God calling his people to settle or to stay stuck in one place or one way of doing things.

> **IT'S BECAUSE YOU'RE STUCK IN DESTRUCTIVE THINKING THAT SO MANY OF YOUR PLANS ARE SINKING.**

Instead, you find God calling people to take more ground and to move forward. I've known too many people who get stuck in a certain way of thinking, a bad habit, or a harmful relationship. Many of us let our pasts or our current situations hold us prisoner. We let the broken dreams of yesterday haunt us and keep us frozen in place. But this viewpoint only prevents us from moving forward. It's because you're stuck in destructive thinking that so many of your plans are sinking. If you truly want to grab hold of your God-given potential, it starts with movement.

GROW IT, STIR IT, FAN IT

When it comes to faith, we can't remain stagnant. In Paul's second letter to Timothy, the young disciple he was mentoring, he opened with this statement:

I am reminded of your sincere faith, which first lived in your grandmother Lois and in your mother Eunice and, I am persuaded, now lives in you also.

For this reason I remind you to fan into flame the gift of God, which is in you through the laying on of my hands. (1:5–6)

First, Paul talked about Timothy's grandmother and mother and commented on their great faith. He told Timothy about the faith of Lois and Eunice. (I mean, can you get any more perfect grandma names? I want them to knit me some stockings and cook me a meatloaf.) Then he called Timothy not to be sedentary about this faith.

He was saying, "Don't just sit around because your family has faith. That's not enough to carry you. You need to do something about the gift inside of you."

Then he called Timothy to move, saying, "Fan into flame the gift of God," showing that faith is something you have to work at. The New King James Version says it this way: "Therefore I remind you to stir up the gift of God which is in you through the laying on of my hands."

It's not enough to have faith for only one day. It's not enough to rely on the faith of others like Lois and Eunice. You have to work at this thing every day. You have to fan it and pursue it.

Think of faith like a dish at a buffet. When I was growing up, my parents often took our family to a place called the Golden Corral. Forget the Old Country Buffet, the Golden Corral was where it was at. We'd go there almost every Sunday after church and terrorize the place.

I remember walking through the buffet line and looking at some of the dishes. Sometimes the casserole or macaroni looked like it had been sitting there for two or more hours. A filmy layer of nastiness sat on the top and let you know, "This thing hasn't been touched in a while." As a middle school boy, I was never deterred by this.

I would give that filmy layer one look and say, "Give me that spoon." Then I'd start stirring up the dish. The more I stirred, the fresher it looked. After about thirty seconds, the nastiness was gone and it looked brand-new!

Our faith is a lot like that dish at the Golden Corral. If we never put any energy into it, if we don't daily ask God for things, or daily convince ourselves of his existence and purpose, then it starts to grow stale. But if we take the time to stir it up like Paul called Timothy to do, we start to transition out of our own dream and disappointment and into God's plan. We start to look, act, and move a little differently.

STRETCH IT OUT

In Mark 3, we meet a man who found himself stale and stuck in his circumstances. Because of a condition that left his hand withered and disfigured, he was an outcast. He entered the world already broken. His physical condition affected every part of his life. Without functioning hands, how could he work and make a livelihood? How could he have a family and provide for them? How could he dream up a future for himself? His hand affected him socially, physically, and financially. His situation was bleak, but what made it worse was the fact that he wasn't even allowed into a church building.

This wasn't America. There was no such thing as the "land of opportunity" for this guy. I'm sure he thought he would always remain in his hopeless situation, shunned because of his physical condition.

But then Jesus came along. All the leaders of the church were there and waiting for Jesus to do something wrong. Remember, this was a generation of faithless skeptics. "Some of them were looking for a reason to accuse Jesus, so they watched him closely to see if he would heal him on the Sabbath" (Mark 3:2). They were ready to make their move. They were waiting for the slip-up that would finally end Jesus' ministry. Because Jesus came to disrupt the law and the old way of doing things, the scribes and Pharisees weren't big fans. Jesus could've lain low, but instead he decided to call out our friend with the withered hand. "Jesus said to the man . . . 'Stand up in front of everyone'" (v. 3).

If I were this man, sitting on the outskirts, just hoping no one noticed me, I would probably be upset with Jesus at that moment. I would probably be thinking, *For real? Everybody knows I'm the man with the withered hand, and you're going to call me out in front of them!* I'm sure he'd been made fun of his whole life and assumed that Jesus was going to make a spectacle of him, just as so many others had done before. But something different was about to happen.

After Jesus called the man out, he looked to the religious leaders and asked, "Do you think it's okay to heal this guy or not?" Speaking to the spirit of religion and to people who wanted to put God in a box, Jesus asked them, "Which is lawful on the Sabbath: to do good or to do evil, to save life or to kill?" (v. 4).

Many of us try to put God in a box like these teachers did. But God will always surprise you with who he loves, who he calls forward, and who he brings to the dinner party. Because he is

God, he can do whatever he wants, whenever he wants, with whomever he wants.

And in this moment, Jesus wanted to heal this man with the withered hand.

He looked at the judging eyes around him and basically said, "Let me ask you a question. Here is a man stuck in his infirmity, who's struggled his whole life with this terrible condition! Do you think I can heal him or not?"

The man encountered Jesus on a day when he was completely fed up with religion. Filled with frustration, Jesus turned to the man and said, "Stretch out your hand" (v. 5).

I'm sure the man's internal dialogue went something like this: *First, you called me out in front of these people. Now you want me to bring out the thing that embarrasses me the most and show it to everyone? We're talking about the thing they've ridiculed me about my whole life! The reason they treat me like an outcast!*

If I were the man, I might've given up right then and there. *Uh-uh. Not gonna happen*, is what I would be thinking. But the man didn't give up. Though he was asked to extend his shame, he didn't shrink away. When Jesus asked him to stretch out his hand, he took the first step of faith that we've been talking about. He opened his arm, he extended his hand, and the moment he did, "his hand was completely restored" (Mark 3:5). Once he made that move, God blessed him. This is a lesson we could all stand to learn. If you're not willing to stretch it out, you're saying, "I'm good with missing out."

> **IF YOU'RE NOT WILLING TO STRETCH IT OUT, YOU'RE SAYING, "I'M GOOD WITH MISSING OUT."**

GOD ALWAYS CALLS US FORWARD

What I love about this story in Mark is how Jesus called the man to make the move that would ultimately pull him out of his circumstances. He said, "Stretch out the thing that needs me the most. Give me the part of your life that you're ashamed of. Stretch out your failure and your shortcomings, and watch what I do."

As we discussed when we talked about heart rather than perfection, God loves you just the way you are. But he loves you way too much to leave you that way. Like the man with the withered hand, he wants us to make the move toward him. And he wants us to make that move regardless of our mistakes or shortcomings.

But it takes faith to make such a bold move. The man in the story didn't just listen to Jesus. He didn't merely think to himself, *Oh, what a nice thought. "Stretch out your hand." I'm going to write that in my journal tomorrow morning over coffee.* Jesus said, "Stretch out your hand!" and the man could've said, "No! Absolutely not!" He could've chosen to hide that withered piece of himself. He could've kept this shameful side of him a secret, tucked away from the world. But he didn't.

In the Greek language this story was originally written in, the word Mark used to describe the man's hand means "dried up." How would you react if Jesus asked you to stretch out the part of your life that is most dried up? What if he asked you to expose your crushed hopes and wishes, your soul, your marriage, your health, your struggles with anxiety, your loneliness, or your regret? Would you only listen and remain stagnant? Would you say, "No way! I'm out!"?

Or would you do what the man with the withered hand did? When Jesus called him to move, he did just that. He extended his hand with trust and confidence, displaying his faith in Jesus. He believed that if Jesus was the one who was calling him out to do this embarrassing thing, his life would turn out better than it had started. He could put all his trust, all his heart, and all his strength in Jesus.

Faith is not only an attitude; it's also an action. It's never a language or specific way of saying a prayer or talking about a situation. Rather, it's something that shows itself in the steps you take and the decisions you make every day. This man's action was stretching out his imperfection toward God. That took confidence and trust in God's transforming power. That action brought him into God's greater future—a life of healing. What will your action be?

TWO STEPS FORWARD, NO STEPS BACK

Growing up, I loved listening to Paula Abdul. This was way before the *American Idol* era, way back when Arsenio Hall and Magic Johnson were the epitome of cool. She was killing it back in those days. She had a little song called "Opposites Attract"[3] and a music video with a weird animated cat (but we won't get into all that). My favorite part of the song was the chorus, when Paula sang, "I take two steps forward. I take two steps back." (If that is now stuck in your head, you're welcome.)

In my life as a pastor, I've seen too many people in church who live out the lyrics of this song. They take two steps forward, stretch out a dried-up part of their lives, make a decision for Jesus, choose to give up their plans for his, and then end up taking two steps right back. The result? An immobile life. These

121

people could be walking into their best possible tomorrows, but they can't seem to move forward.

The gospel, God's story and good news, is all about movement.

- "Come, follow me" (Matthew 4:19).
- "Go now and leave your life of sin" (John 8:11).
- "Stretch out your hand" (Mark 3:5).

Follow. Go. Stretch. It's clear that faith without movement is dead. I think it's time we ignore Paula's words. Let's take two steps forward and no steps back!

What happens when we take these two steps forward?

The best part about the story of the man with the withered hand is that the instant the man moved, Jesus moved right along with him and restored his broken body. As soon as the man took action, God was ready to bring him into a new future and reality. You must realize that God can't move until you move. The ball's in your court.

GOD CAN'T MOVE UNTIL YOU MOVE. THE BALL'S IN YOUR COURT.

He's waiting for us to stretch out our weaknesses so that he can stretch out his hand to change us. We often get frustrated because we're just sitting around, waiting for God to move in our lives.

"God, when will you pull me out of this circumstance?"
"God, when will you heal this person?"
"God, when can I accomplish all my hopes and dreams?"
"God, when will you give me that job?"

"God, when will you change things for me?"

The funny thing about questions like these is that God is waiting for us to move! It isn't the other way around.

I think the greatest step of faith found in the Bible occurred when Jesus died on the cross for us. Because of this movement and Jesus' confidence that God's plan was the right plan, he saved the world. Did he look back? Did he step off the cross? No! He took two steps forward and no steps back. And because he did, we're still singing about it today.

LET'S MOVE INTO OUR TOMORROW

I get excited when I think about you, reader, because I truly believe that you're on the brink of God's amazing plan for your life. I know that you, like all of us, have experienced the bitter reality when things don't happen in the timing or in the way you had hoped. But despite this, there's no question whether you have a future. The greatness of your life is ridiculous and unparalleled. Remember the words of Isaiah 64:4: "No one has heard, no ear has perceived, no eye has seen any God besides you, who acts on behalf of those who wait for him."

But you'll never step into that ridiculous potential until you throw off the things that keep you stagnant and have faith to move forward into all God has for you.

You might be trying to hide the flaws you have like the man tried in the Mark 3 story. Or maybe you're clinging to the past and beating yourself up because of the mistakes you've made like Jonah did. Don't hold on to your history at the expense of your destiny.

It's time to let go of the broken dreams in your life so that you can grab hold of all God has in store for you and move forward in faith. Only then can we take those two steps out of our current circumstance and forward into God's future.

Years ago, my favorite football team, the Seattle Seahawks, had a terrible record. We never should have made it to the playoffs, but because our whole division was so bad, we found ourselves there. When we were about to face the New Orleans Saints on our home field, no one thought the outcome would be pretty. The fans were prepared to lose, but go down fighting.

Little did we realize that we had just acquired a new weapon: the running back from the Buffalo Bills, Marshawn Lynch. We like to call him "Beast Mode," because he's an absolute beast. With his famous play, the "Beast Quake," he shook our entire city. I remember watching this game and finding myself in awe at Lynch's technique. Three guys started to tackle him, but instead of admitting defeat and falling to the ground, Lynch just kept moving. The entire game he just kept moving his legs and throwing people off of him. The whole thing looked like a video game, and Seattle was going crazy. Finally, Lynch got to the end zone and fell down. He had been running for what to me felt like fifteen minutes! I just about lost my mind watching this crazy play go down. He changed everything for the Seahawks.

It's all because he had made the decision to keep moving forward no matter what came against him. What stops you from moving forward like this? Is it sin, maybe something you've been struggling with? Is it a symptom, maybe an emotion, or something you need healing from? Is it someone, maybe a friend who's dragging you down?

If you're pragmatic and looking for your next steps when it comes to moving forward in faith, start by asking those questions. Then . . .

If the answer is sin . . .

Talk to someone. "Confess your sins to each other and pray for each other so that you may be healed" (James 5:16). Sin doesn't have to destroy your life. Silence about your sin will.

> SIN DOESN'T HAVE TO DESTROY YOUR LIFE. SILENCE ABOUT YOUR SIN WILL.

If the answer is a symptom . . .

See a doctor. Talk to a therapist or counselor. Reach out to a small group leader or pastor. Buy a gym membership, and get your blood flowing. Figure out the root problem, and start your road to recovery. Don't think ignoring it will make it go away.

If the answer is someone . . .

Yes, we're called to live at peace with everyone. But we can also love somebody from afar. We don't have to be close with everyone, especially not those who are toxic. If someone is keeping you from moving forward in your faith, it may be time to cut them out. Delete phone numbers; block them on social media; do whatever it takes.

These suggestions may seem oddly practical for something as radical as moving forward into the future God has for you, but this is what it takes. And to truly walk in faith you need to keep moving. No matter what comes against you, you must keep stretching out your imperfections to God, keep stirring, fanning, and growing your faith, and keep throwing off the enemy's plan to hold you back.

Let's press on toward the amazing prize God has set before us. Let's move so God can move.

Chapter Ten
IT'S ALL ABOUT THE FOLLOW

In 2015, the Internet brought us a little treasure in the form of a hip-hop artist–record producer turned Snapchat motivational speaker. His name? DJ Khaled. While others used Snapchat's twenty-four-hour story feature to put dog filters on their faces or document their trips to Coachella, DJ Khaled decided to turn it into a platform for positivity.

If you haven't seen his snaps, let me paint you a picture. Usually you find Khaled at his house, watering his plants or getting a massage by his pool. While he invites you into a day in the life, he also gives you his simple "keys to success."

"Find peace. Life is like a waterfall. You gotta flow," he says as he shows you a video of water flowing into a pond with a praying hands emoji. It's groundbreaking stuff.

"The key to success is using the right soap," he says as he stands in his shower with a phone. (I wonder how many phones he's ruined because of water damage.) "I only use Dove," he proclaims while waving the bar of soap at the screen. "Dove soap! Trust me! The key to success!"

"Cocoa butter is the key to success."

"Manicure and pedicure once a week. MAJOR key to success."

As he waters plants, he tells you, "Major key. Never panic. Don't panic."

"Surround yourself with angels. Positive energy. Beautiful people. Beautiful souls. Clean hearts. The keys to success."

These are just some of the thousands of keys that DJ Khaled shares with all of us via his snaps. And actually I am a big fan. Once I ran into him at a basketball game, and I couldn't help myself. I usually try to play it cool around big names, but I had to tell him I loved his work. "Hey, man!" I said. "Thank you so much for inspiring people!"

There's something pretty awesome about a force of positivity in today's negative world, even if that positivity does come in the form of soap suggestions and cocoa butter lathering.

Although I look forward to Khaled's daily pep talks and tips, I think he's missing one very important key to success. He most likely hasn't included it because it's not that common today in a world where everyone wants to be a leader, to be the next big thing, or to pave the way.

PERHAPS OUR BIGGEST FEAR IS NOT THE UNKNOWN BUT RATHER THE DECISION TO FOLLOW.

The real key to success?

Following.

If movement is important to God, then you may be wondering, *What move should I make now? What's the most important next step? How does this whole thing play out?* We've talked about getting rid of the sin, symptom, or someone who is getting in your way. But I believe that the most crucial movement when it comes to walking in God's plan is the follow.

Every day you must make a choice to follow Jesus. It's when you follow him that you begin to walk in true success, and God's plan for your life unfolds. But this isn't easy. This means abandoning your own thing, your own plan, and your own dreams. Perhaps our biggest fear is not the unknown but rather the decision to follow.

THE ORIGINAL FOLLOWERS

Let's go back to where this idea of following all began.

> As Jesus was walking beside the Sea of Galilee, he saw two brothers, Simon called Peter and his brother Andrew. They were casting a net into the lake, for they were fishermen. "Come, follow me," Jesus said, "and I will send you out to fish for people." At once they left their nets and followed him.
>
> Going on from there, he saw two other brothers, James son of Zebedee and his brother John. They were in a boat with their father Zebedee, preparing their nets. Jesus called them, and immediately they left the boat and their father and followed him. (Matthew 4:18–22)

In this story, we see two sets of brothers going about their daily lives: James and John, and Peter and Andrew. Jesus said the same thing to both, revealing just how important this concept of following really is to their stories.

"Come, follow me."

As we've already covered, Simon Peter didn't hesitate after hearing these words. Once his brother, Andrew, discovered Jesus and quickly ran to tell him all about it, together they made the decision to drop their occupations and their nets, along with everything that was comfortable and familiar for them. They left it all on the boat and said, "Okay. I'm going to follow that guy."

James and John did the same, even choosing to leave their own father in the boat!

You have to be really excited about what's to come to leave your dad to do all the work. You know when you're a kid and your dad makes you do a "house project" with him? He's got all the tools laid out, he's ready for this amazing father-son bonding moment, and then one of your friends hits you up to go to the park. When I was young, I always felt terrible about abandoning Pops for my friends. I knew if I dropped my fence-building gear or paintbrush, and said, "Peace out!" to my dad, I would feel terrible at the dinner table that night. And I knew my dad would most likely lay the guilt on thick.

But a dad guilt trip didn't keep James or John from dropping everything and following Jesus. They said good-bye to their family, and off they went to see what this man was all about.

We also see Jesus making this same ask of Levi, the tax collector, in Luke 5. "After this, Jesus went out and saw a tax collector by the name of Levi sitting at his tax booth. 'Follow me,' Jesus said to him, and Levi got up, left everything and followed him" (vv. 27–28).

This pattern continues throughout the Gospels as Jesus gathers his twelve disciples like he's walking around Galilee rounding up the Avengers for some major showdown. And each time the story goes something like this:

Jesus says, "Follow me."

The disciple says, "Cool. Will do," drops what he's doing, and follows.

It's not like Jesus walked up to these guys with a big speech. He didn't roll up in a fancy car and say, "If you follow me, I'm going to give you houses, money, fame, coffee with cream, the LA Rams. You name it, you get it." He made no bold promises of instant success. He simply said, "Follow me."

> **A FOLLOW TODAY COULD LEAD TO A LEGACY TOMORROW.**

I find this so fascinating. It proves that there was something about Jesus in these moments that drew these men toward him. There was something about him that made them want to leave everything behind. Something about Jesus gave Peter, Andrew, James, John, Levi, and the others faith and confidence. And though it didn't start with a long list of promises from Jesus, God did end up giving them a better future. Because they followed, they got to walk into a reality far better than new houses, money, or fame.

Remember, it's the disciples who started the revival. It's the disciples who built the church. They would go down in the history books, shake up the world, and spread Christianity! They made the decision to trust and leave everything, and today you and I know Jesus' story and what it means to be a part of God's church and plan because of them.

And it all started with a follow. A follow today could lead to a legacy tomorrow.

WHAT DOES IT MEAN TO FOLLOW?

How do we follow like the disciples followed? How do we make this movement toward Jesus so that we can also be world changers, walking in God's plan?

First, we know from the disciples' stories that we need to lay everything aside and find our complete identity in Jesus. Jesus is the object, remember? This means that he's worth giving up our families, homes, and means of income for.

Before you quit your job, delete your family members from your phone contacts, and live in a cardboard box, hear me out. This kind of total abandonment to Jesus' will doesn't look the same for every person. God might be calling you to stay at your job or move closer to your family. The key is finding out where he's going, where he wants you to go, and then start following.

Jesus does not hate good jobs, money, career success, or family. But the moment these things become more important to you than he is, you're missing the whole point.

If your job, your family, or your salary are the key factors in your decision making, you're not really following Jesus; you're following things. This means you're living out your plan and not God's. We need to pray like Jesus prayed. Before he died on the cross for the sins of the world, he said to God, "Father, if you are willing, take this cup from me; yet not my will, but yours be done" (Luke 22:42). We need to live out God's will. Jesus knew that God's plan was better than his plan.

Second, following looks like modeling your actions after Jesus' actions. The disciples were sent out by Jesus to do his work. And this work involved spreading his truth and the message of his grace and love. Jesus' final words were, "Go and make disciples" (Matthew 28:19). "Find more people to follow me. Help others discover their God-given potential. Heal the sick.

Teach others to obey these commandments that will alter their lives for the better."

When we're really following Jesus, we're living out this mission too. We're not only walking in our best possible tomorrow, but we're helping those around us walk in it too. We're meant to share in the same mission Jesus had: to change the world!

Last, following means joining Jesus in bearing your own cross every day. Now, this might sound weird to you if you didn't grow up going to church or have never popped open a Bible.

Okay, Chad. You want me to die on a cross?

Like Jesus?

Like be tortured and kill myself?

Wait, what?

You're probably thinking something along these lines, and I'm sure you're terrified. But this is not what Jesus meant.

When Jesus asked his followers to "take up their cross" (Mark 8), he didn't mean for them to do the literal act of dying. I think he explains it best, so let's let Jesus' words speak for themselves:

> "WHAT GOOD IS IT FOR SOMEONE TO GAIN THE WHOLE WORLD, YET FORFEIT THEIR SOUL?"
> —JESUS

Whoever wants to be my disciple must deny themselves and take up their cross and follow me. For whoever wants to save their life will lose it, but whoever loses their life for me and for the gospel will save it. What good is it for someone to gain the whole world, yet forfeit their soul? (vv. 34–36)

Following with faith means denying our own selfish desires, giving up our own plans, and replacing our agendas with God's. I love that question Jesus asked his followers. What good is it if we have millions of fans, the biggest house, or the hottest Snapchat account? What good is it if we succeed in all our dreams and make it according to the world's standards?

It means nothing if we're not following Jesus. It means nothing if we're living in darkness, loneliness, anxiety, or depression. And it truly means nothing if we don't affect the world around us for the better and transform lives with the good news.

I don't know about you, but I'd rather gain Jesus than the whole world. This is why I'm going to make a plan to follow him every day.

HELLO FROM THE OTHER SIDE

In Genesis 22, we see Abraham following God even when it's difficult. Whenever I read this story about a father having to do the unimaginable in response to God, I'm always challenged to take a closer look at my own obedience.

If you're not familiar with the story, Abraham and his wife, Sarah, had waited a long time to have a baby. And God had finally given them Isaac. He was the promise they had been waiting for, and then God dropped a bombshell.

God said, "Take your son, your only son, whom you love— Isaac—and go to the region of Moriah. Sacrifice him there as a burnt offering on a mountain I will show you" (v. 2).

If you were reading *The Hunger Games* right now, this is where you would slam the book shut and say, "Oh, no, you didn't!" If you stopped reading here, you might feel outraged or offended. But to truly understand this story, you need to keep reading.

Abraham followed what God asked him to do even though it wasn't easy. His response was obedience. As he walked up that mountain with his son, he was saying, "God, your plan, not mine. Your future, not my own." At that moment, I'm sure the dream he had for his life with his son was shattered.

And guess what? God's plan was greater and better than Abraham realized! We have to understand that on the other side of his broken dream, God was preparing the actual sacrifice. Abraham couldn't see it at the time of his obedience, but God had a ram waiting on the other side of that mountain. In the end, Abraham wouldn't have to kill his own son. Once he proved his obedience and followed after God, he was shown a better plan in the thicket!

> When they reached the place God had told him about, Abraham built an altar there and arranged the wood on it. He bound his son Isaac and laid him on the altar, on top of the wood. Then he reached out his hand and took the knife to slay his son. But the angel of the LORD called out to him from heaven, "Abraham! Abraham!"
>
> "Here I am," he replied.
>
> "Do not lay a hand on the boy," he said. "Do not do anything to him. Now I know that you fear God, because you have not withheld from me your son, your only son."
>
> Abraham looked up and there in a thicket he saw a ram caught by its horns. He went over and took the ram and sacrificed it as a burnt offering instead of his son. So Abraham called that place The LORD Will Provide. And to this day it is said, "On the mountain of the LORD it will be provided." (vv. 9–14)

What will the Lord provide for you? What could be coming on the other side of your mountain? What's on the other side of your step of obedience? What's on the other side of your follow?

I've never been asked to do something as extreme as sacrifice my own kid. But there have been moments every day when I've had to obey and follow God's plan when it didn't make sense.

On April 10, 1996, at Seattle's Kingdome, I made the choice as a teenager to give up my plan and chase after God's without knowing what would be on the other side of that choice. I grew up a Christian, fully immersed in the church world, with two amazing parents. My crazy Mexican mom and extremely white dad did a pretty good job making God a reality in my life. And I truly loved him. I loved the Bible, I loved the church community, and I loved the Holy Spirit. But I was also following my own plan.

I may not have been living an outward life of obvious sins, but I was still just "doing me." My life was all about my dreams, my needs, and my idea of where I should be heading. And even though I loved God, the church, and the Bible, I was far from the future God had in store for me.

I was sixteen years old when I went to a men's event called Promise Keepers. I'll never forget walking into that giant stadium and seeing sixty-five thousand men of all ages fill the seats. I was sitting way up on the 300 level, behind the stage, and the whole stadium was singing a hymn. It was during the booming chorus that I felt something change inside of me. Call it a turning point. Call it a decisive moment. Whatever it was, it made a huge difference in my life.

I remember lifting my hands as a sign of surrender and saying to God, "I'm going to say yes to your plan and your dream for my life, God." Something inside of me was drawing me toward a better life. And from that moment on, I started to follow.

At the age of eighteen, I chose to follow again. I followed God to LA, unsure of how it would affect my future. And I followed him back to Seattle at twenty-four. Then back again to LA at thirty-four. Each of these big steps took faith and confidence that God had something better on the other side. But there were also a thousand little steps in between. There were small moments in the day when I followed his leading to call someone I hadn't talked to in a while or wake up early to study something I hadn't before. There were many moments of failures that delayed God's blessing and plan, but also moments of his mercy as he continued to give me another chance.

And each time I followed and obeyed, I discovered that the other side of the mountain always looked much better than what I had in mind.

WHAT HAPPENS WHEN WE FOLLOW?

If we want to understand better what happens when we make the decision to walk out our faith by following Jesus, let's look again to the disciples' story. Because they followed, Peter and the gang weren't just Jesus' pupils, they were his friends. Their relationship was deep and meaningful.

In John 13, after they'd shared a meal together, Jesus decided to show this level of friendship by humbling himself and washing their feet. I love Peter's reaction here. As I already told you, I am not a big fan of the way my feet look. (Let's just say, if socks with sandals were cool, I'd be wearing them every day.) I think Peter felt the same way, because when Jesus knelt to wash his feet, Peter's response was a little something like this:

"No."

"Nope."

"Not gonna happen."

He said, "You shall never wash my feet" (v. 8). (Peter obviously didn't have DJ Khaled telling him the key to success was in the pedi.)

But Jesus insisted, and even though he is the Son of God, their leader and teacher, he bowed low to the ground, took off their sandals, and washed their feet. What a beautiful picture of intimacy and friendship. This is the kind of intimacy we have access to if we start following! Jesus wants to take care of us, wash us clean, and get down on our level. He wants us to expose our nasty feet, or the ugliest part of us, and, in return, he wants to show us his acceptance, love, and transforming power.

Jesus didn't view his followers as slaves or students. He viewed them as friends, the same way he views us. Jesus said, "I no longer call you servants, because a servant does not know his master's business. Instead, I have called you friends, for everything that I learned from my Father I have made known to you" (John 15:15).

I think friendship with Jesus is one of the greatest rewards we can achieve and is part of this grand plan of God's we've been talking about all along. When we follow, we can walk in this friendship, as well as a world-changing future, just like Peter and the other disciples did. We could even be used to build Christ's church like they were.

It's time to stop trying to be the leader over your life. Stop trying to be in complete control of your future. Don't walk around each day trying to manipulate and force things into existence. If you do, you'll find yourself in some career you don't want with relationships you don't want, completely miserable.

So often I thank God that I didn't end up becoming that coach and teacher I wanted to be when I was in high school. I know that my own plan would've led me to a sad, unsatisfying life. Not because there's anything inherently sad about those paths, but because they weren't what God made me to be.

If the key to success is following Jesus, it's time to stop leaning on your own understanding and start sitting with God. We start this by telling him, "I want to be a follower. I choose to lay my life down for you. I'm ready to leave everything behind. I'm willing to abandon what I'm familiar and comfortable with. I don't care about what makes me popular or famous. I care about your plan."

And as you follow every day, God will begin to make his perfect will available to you. Remember, he's not about the spoilers. He won't show you every single thing he has in store for you. But as you follow and obey, he'll unfold a little bit more of the story each day. "The path of the righteous is like the morning sun, *shining ever brighter till the full light of day*" (Proverbs 4:18, emphasis added). Every step you take in obedience to God's

> **EXCHANGE YOUR STRIVING AFTER SUCCESS FOR RESTING IN YOUR SAVIOR.**

plan will make things brighter, clearer, and more abundant. Exchange your striving after success for resting in your Savior.

5 TAKEAWAYS

Are you ready to walk out this plan with faith? Are you ready to follow the real person of Jesus? Are you willing to drop everything and move toward a God who is bigger and better than your own plans and dreams? Are you ready to make the Big Ask?

I often meet Christians who find this idea—walking out something so impractical as faith—confusing. How do you do faith? How do you live out a belief in someone you can't physically see or touch? We've already covered the importance of asking, moving, and following, but I wanted to leave you with five additional next steps for walking out this faith journey:

1. Identify your first step.

    Write down a first step and actually take it. It could look like leaving something or someone behind. It could also look like forgiving someone for past pain they've caused you. Colossians 3:13 says to "forgive as the Lord forgave you." You have to be convinced about God's grace toward you so that you can extend it to those around you. This takes faith.

2. Stop believing for everyone but yourself.

As I've mentioned, it's easy for us to believe in the best for others. We have no problem asking God for big things when it comes to our friends and loved ones. And there's nothing wrong with that! You should be asking and believing for others. But don't forget to believe for yourself too.

3. Be a great follower.

Following is something we have to cultivate and work at. Write these questions down, along with your best answers.

- What can I start doing today to become a follower?
- How can I follow closer?
- How can I learn more about where Jesus is going and take steps toward that place?

If you come to God willing to hear the answers to these questions, he'll show you the way.

4. Trust that God is moving in your life.

From 1 (low) to 5 (high), rate your trust in God when it comes to the following areas:

- Dreams/Aspirations
- Finances
- Relationships
- Health

If any of your numbers come out lower than 3, you may want to adjust your thinking in those areas. Remember, God is always on the move. He is active, willing, and ready to do great things in and through you.

5. Keep the end in mind.

We aren't taking faith steps forward for our personal success alone. The end game here isn't our names in shining lights. That was your broken dream, remember? We are taking faith steps so that we can receive a greater understanding of God's love and grace! Knowing and having a better understanding of Jesus Christ is the end goal.

Part Four
THE JOURNEY
Where do you turn in the middle?

Chapter Eleven
THE MESS IN THE MIDDLE

A few years ago, my mom came to me with a request on her birthday. My mother is a beautiful Mexican woman full of spice. (She's full, I'm half, and I'm proud.) She is also a runner, which I've always had a hard time understanding. "Mom, you've crossed the border," I often tease her. "You can stop running now. You live in Seattle. You have your green card. You're good." I think I simply don't understand long-distance running in general. What's the point? What team are you on? Don't you people get bored?

Because of this, I surprised even myself when I agreed to my mother's birthday request that year. I sat down with her on the big day and said, "Mom, I'll get you anything you want. What is it you'd like for your birthday?" When I asked this question, I was imagining I would have her hop on Amazon, point at a product, and then I'd click "Add to Cart." But that's not how it went down.

She looked at me with those caring eyes, the ones that had lovingly kept me alive for the first eighteen years of my life. (And that's exactly what those eyes were saying: "I lovingly kept you alive the first eighteen years of your life, so you will give me what I want for my birthday.") Then she started with her request: "This year I want you to run a half marathon with me."

Hold the phone. What? I was ready to run for the door. But I thought it over for a moment. I thought about how fast, or rather, slow my mom runs.

I looked at those eyes again. I couldn't say no.

Because I'm a good son, I agreed. I figured those 13.1 miles are a breeze when you're basically walking and you have the legs of a gazelle like I do.

The race happened to be on Thanksgiving weekend on an extremely cold Sunday morning. I met my mom at the hotel where she was staying in downtown Seattle. I showed up with all my gear on. I had my Nikes, my armband, my iPod with my playlist all queued up, and my headphones. I was ready to walk-run 13.1 miles and make Mama happy.

We were heading out the door to join the other racers when my mom stopped me. "Son, you can't bring your headphones and music. They don't allow those at these races."

Wait.

Hold the phone . . . again.

What now?

Apparently wearing headphones puts racers in danger of getting hit by a car. However, I found it hard to believe that it would be legal to let people run twenty-six miles with no music. I wondered if this was actually some sort of mom ploy to get me to talk to her the entire run instead of listen to my jams.

Because I know how to honor authority and obey my elders, I did as she told me. I left my armband, I left my music, and I left my headphones. I sang them the chorus of Boyz II Men's "It's So

Hard to Say Goodbye to Yesterday," and we headed out to the race.

Before I arrived at the marathon, I had no idea what exactly I had signed up for. I knew my mom did this every year at Thanksgiving, but I thought it was more of a Ma and Pa trot around the city. I didn't realize I would be running alongside twenty thousand other people, some of whom were hardcore racers. It wasn't until my mom and I pulled up and I saw the giant crowd that I realized what I had gotten into. This was the Rock 'n' Roll Marathon, one of the biggest races in Seattle and a huge event put on in cities nationwide.

I had planned on running alongside my mom during the entire race, but when I saw the booming speakers, the athletes all geared up, and the twenty thousand people everywhere, I immediately switched gears. This was a competition. *Deuces, Mom. I'm out. I don't know what your time is going to be, but I know what my time is going to be,* I thought to myself as my mental gears started shifting into athlete mode. I was certain I would be beating everyone that day.

So, naturally, I began to do some serious stretching. I had to get those hammies loose and intimidate my competitors. This was no longer about my mom's birthday; this was about my pride. I was ready to go for it with all I had.

I'll never forget the moment that I heard "Ready. Set. Go!" over the booming speakers. I put those gazelle legs to work and bolted. The first mile was the fastest I have ever run. I felt like I was floating in the air. With twenty thousand people by my side, I felt the adrenaline of the whole event rushing through my veins. It was incredible!

And the ending was equally incredible. When you end this

half marathon in Seattle, the finish line is like a huge arena. Hundreds of fans are cheering you on as they say your name through the speakers. I felt like Prefontaine and Usain Bolt when I ran through. As my foot crossed that finish line, I was convinced the television cameras were on me. I waved at all my fans and looked around for the TV reporters who obviously wanted to interview me. (I didn't ever find them. We won't get into that.)

But I'm not writing this story to tell you about the start of the race or the end of the race, though both were noteworthy. No, it's time to get real about the most challenging portion of all. Let's talk about the middle of the race.

FAITH FOR THE MIDDLE

When you're on mile nine of a half marathon with no head-phones and all you can hear is your own heavy breathing, that's when you find out what you're really made of. This point in the journey feels a little bit different from the starting line and definitely contrasts with the finish line. Your mind goes to an obscure place.

When I was on mile nine, I started thinking about girls who had broken my heart, the tests I had flunked, and the coaches who hadn't given me enough play time. When I was pounding my feet to the pavement with no music or podcast keeping me going, I contemplated calling it quits.

This is because the beginning of something is inspirational. And the end is fulfilling. But the middle? That's where you're put to the test.

We've established that God has an amazing plan for everyone, not just the select few. We've also examined that it takes faith to walk out this plan every day and move past the failures of our past. Now let's look at where this plan will take you. Is God's plan pointing you toward one epic moment? Is this all about one big event where it all comes together for you?

I'm sorry to tell you the answer is no. God's plan is a journey—one with ups and downs. He wants you to live it out at the beginning, the middle, and the end.

I could've shown up to that race, experienced the hype and adrenaline of that first mile, and then peaced out and gone home to my iPod and headphones. But I never would've known the thrill of crossing the finish line. I also could've jumped in with the other runners at mile twelve, run the last mile, and finished in front of a group of screaming fans. But it would've felt pointless had I not run the rest of the race.

Walking in God's plan is like my Rock 'n' Roll marathon experience (except you're allowed to wear headphones). Many of us start chasing after God's dream for our lives with excitement and we're over the moon when God fulfills a promise he made, but God wants to give us the kind of faith that helps us persevere through the middle of this journey, the part that is hard and not always exciting.

> "HE'S NOT ONLY THE AUTHOR AND FINISHER OF MY FAITH; HE'S THE GOD IN THE MIDDLE OF MY FAITH."

How do you continue to pursue God's will for your life in the middle of your struggle? Do you still smile when your legs get heavy and you're short of breath? Do you continue when you're exhausted and want to quit? God's plan is for you to persevere through this portion too. What he's taking you on is a journey of trust. When you find yourself in the murky middle, repeat these words: "He's not only the author and finisher of my faith; he's the God in the middle of my faith."

DESTINED FOR GREATNESS

Let's talk about another hero, or rather antihero, who had a difficult time with the middle of the journey. Let's just say he made a mess of it. In Judges 13, we meet this man, Samson, who was destined for greatness but struggled in the middle portion of his life.

Only four times throughout all the Scripture does an angel of the Lord appear to a parent and say, "Your kid is about to be somebody." We read about it in the stories of Isaac, John the Baptist, Jesus Christ himself, and Samson.

Samson's parents were visited by an angel of the Lord. The angel told them that their son would one day become a deliverer. This is every parent's dream to hear that their child could be somebody. Whether we admit it or not, we all are secretly crazy stage moms. We all want our kids to achieve greatness and believe the best for them.

To understand the promise Samson's parents received, you need to understand that Samson's parents were Israelites. At this point in the story, Israel, God's chosen people, was under the oppressive rule of the Philistines. And it wasn't the first time. Seven times they had found themselves under another nation's terrifying leadership, and this time around God chose Samson to be the deliverer. Before he was even born, God selected him to save a whole people group.

When the angel spoke to Samson's parents, he started getting very specific, telling them some conditions to their son's greatness. The angel said, "You will become pregnant and have a son whose head is never to be touched by a razor because the boy is to be a Nazirite, dedicated to God from the womb. He will take the lead in delivering Israel from the hands of the Philistines" (v. 5).

I'm sure at this moment Samson's parents were both over-the-moon excited and thoroughly confused. *Our child will be a deliverer. Okay, loving that,* they probably thought. *But what's this now about not cutting his hair?*

Samson's hair would be the secret to his sauce, the key to his purpose. If he was truly going to deliver his people, he'd have to keep the man bun. One cut of his hair, and the strength would leave him. But what's an odd command here or there when greatness is being spoken over your life?

Before we dive into Samson's messy middle and the pitfalls he fell into, let's fast-forward to the happy ending. Because we all love a good Disney movie, where the boy gets the girl, the team wins the game, and everyone hugs each other, I will give you a glimpse of Samson's finale.

Despite the catastrophe he would ultimately find himself in, he would go down as a hero in Hebrews 11. Remember, this is the Hall of Faith. This is where we recount the stories of those great men and women who possessed inspiring faith. This is where we can find Samson.

"What more shall I say?" the author asked in Hebrews 11:32. After listing the many throughout the Bible who accomplished great things because of faith, he then continued the list:

I do not have time to tell about Gideon, Barak, Samson and Jephthah, about David and Samuel and the prophets, who through faith conquered kingdoms, administered justice, and gained what was promised; who shut the mouth of lions, quenched the fury of the flames, and escaped the edge of the sword; whose weakness was turned to strength; and who became powerful in battle and routed foreign armies. (vv. 32–34)

That, right there, is greatness. That passage, which usually makes me picture a scene from *Braveheart*, tells of what happens when people choose to walk in faith and into God's plan for their lives. Samson would go down in this hall of fame because he eventually fulfilled the call of God. In the end, he defeated foreign enemies and conquered kingdoms. He did exactly what God said he would!

Samson's beginning was amazing. Angels revealed themselves to his parents. Promise was spoken over his life. And his end was spectacular. The Philistines were defeated. The Israelites were delivered. But the middle of his story, like many of ours, came with its own set of unique challenges.

DESTINED, BUT DISTRACTED

Because God calls and qualifies an imperfect people, our journey with him doesn't always go as planned. Though he has greatness planned for each of us, we often get sidetracked because of our weaknesses. Bumps in the road exist. Detours in the middle of our marathon confuse us and distract us from the race.

This is what happened to Samson. "Samson went down to Timnah and saw there a young Philistine woman. When he returned, he said to his father and mother, 'I have seen a

Philistine woman in Timnah; now get her for me as my wife'"
(Judges 14:1–2).

Hold up.

Can't you just go fishing in your own pond, Samson?

Let's all remember that the Philistines were the enemies. The
Philistines were the ones Samson was supposed to be delivering
the Israelites from, not falling in love with. He saw what the Lord
had forbidden, what God had said no to, and decided to chase
after it.

Even though he was filled with holy confidence and knew
the plan God had laid out for him, Samson got distracted by his
weakness in the middle of his journey. Though he knew God had
a dream for his life, he went after his own dream instead. *Oh, I'll
go rescue Israel later. Right now this is what I want.*

The same thing happens to many of us on our journeys with
God. We start off with confidence, but often expect God's plan
to happen in an instant. After weeks or years go by without a
complete fulfillment of his promises to us, we start to get distracted. Our weakness trips us up. Instead of having faith every
day and trusting that God will unveil things piece by piece over
time, we meander in the middle of the journey. And it's often to
our own downfall.

Samson was strong about God but weak about women.
What's your weakness? This wasn't the first time women
tripped up Samson on his journey. Maybe you have a similar
weakness for romance. Or maybe you have trouble spending
money you don't have, losing your temper, rebelling, walking
around with a cynical attitude, or finding yourself consumed
with envy. Your dream might be wrapped up in something
God says no to like mine was with my long-distance girlfriend.

Or you might be addicted to the thing that's trying to take you out of the game.

It's important to beware of these weaknesses. Satan will always use them to snare you and keep you from the great life God has planned.

Samson's father tried to talk him out of his terrible decision. "Don't go there, son. That will cost you more than you ever want to pay. That is the enemy's camp. That's what the Lord said no to."

But too distracted by his own weakness, Samson refused to listen. One thing led to another, and there was a wedding. Photographer, suit, best man, maid of honor, dress, flowers, the whole thing. Everyone was posting on Instagram or whatever the Israelite equivalent was. They were celebrating this union between a Philistine and an Israelite. While they were at the feast, Samson told a riddle and promised a great reward if anyone could figure it out.

Then he went home with his new wife, the enemy, and she eventually convinced him to give her the answer to the riddle. Immediately, the whole decision backfired on Samson. Once she knew the answer, his new wife went straight to the other Philistines. They solved it, and this outraged Samson. It made him so angry that "he went down to Ashkelon, struck down thirty of their men, stripped them of everything and gave their clothes to those who had explained the riddle" (Judges 14:19).

As if his wife's betrayal of his trust wasn't enough, verse 20 of the story continues with, "And Samson's wife was given to one of his companions who had attended him at the feast." Oh snap. The girl ran away with one of the groomsmen at the wedding! To make matters even worse, it says that Samson went looking for her. At the start of Judges 15, we read:

Later on, at the time of wheat harvest, Samson took a young goat and went to visit his wife. He said, "I'm going to my wife's room." But her father would not let him go in.

"I was so sure you hated her," he said, "that I gave her to your companion." (vv. 1–2)

Imagine how awful Samson felt at this moment. I'm sure he was beating himself up for letting himself wander from God's plan like that.

His parents were right; he never should have gone there. He let his weakness distract him from God's plan. He strayed in the middle of his journey and paid the price.

Most of our frustrations are tied to our distractions. Often we can't seem to do the big things we feel God has laid out for us because we're letting small things veer us from the path.

> **MOST OF OUR FRUSTRATIONS ARE TIED TO OUR DISTRACTIONS.**

There is a famous inspirational mantra that says, "Starve your distractions and feed your focus."[4] If you're distracted by sex (as Samson was), shallow fame, spending money, or something other than God's dream, starve it. Don't let it keep you from walking in God's plan.

DELUSIONAL IN PAIN

Samson's story, like many of ours, doesn't stop with only one bad decision. After this heartbreaking betrayal by his first wife, he didn't get back on the straight and narrow and pursue God's will for his life. No, at that moment in the story, he was filled with pain and heartache. And this pain prevented him from making the right decisions.

Sometimes our pain, the pain we often bring upon ourselves, causes us to do some dumb things and lose track of our purpose. As we walk out our faith every day and chase after God's plan, we need to look out for distractions that may trip us up or the pain that may prevent us from making wise choices.

Samson, filled with heartache, only returned to his weakness. He went back and did the same thing all over again. He found another Philistine woman, named Delilah, and married her.

> Some time later, he fell in love with a woman in the Valley of Sorek whose name was Delilah. The rulers of the Philistines went to her and said, "See if you can lure him into showing you the secret of his great strength and how we can over-power him so we may tie him up and subdue him. Each one of us will give you eleven hundred shekels of silver." (Judges 16:4–5)

The very foundation of their relationship was built on deception. Delilah's goal was to woo him into giving up his secret. And all for money. How could Samson be so stupid to fall for this trap, especially after he'd already made a similar mistake?

This part of the story always frustrates me, but what's even more frustrating is how it applies to our everyday lives. If we don't get healed from our issues after the first mistake, we're just going to repeat the same thing over and over. If we don't get healed of our destructive thinking or the weaknesses that often trip us up as we walk out this journey, our issues will ultimately take us out of the race entirely.

This is because pain makes you delusional. Have you ever been so injured you lose your judgment? One time I tore all the ligaments in my foot playing basketball. I remember the pain being so excruciating that it consumed my every thought. Because it was always there, pulsing and getting worse, I couldn't think about anything else. If someone asked me a question, it was hard for me to even form a reply. My foot was all I could think about. My injury prevented me from moving forward.

Your world might be so full of pain that it's hard to even make a sound, wise decision. It's hard to know what sort of path or unimaginable life God has called you to because only one thing consumes your every thought: pain. Samson was betrayed, he lost his wife, and what did he do? He ran back to repeat the whole thing again.

If you are to walk in greatness, don't give up the first time you experience pain like this. Pain will happen in all our lives. In fact, I guarantee it. Our job is to get healed of that pain so we can step toward our destiny and God-given potential. Say to yourself, "I cannot make contemporary decisions based upon historical pain."

"I CANNOT MAKE CONTEMPORARY DECISIONS BASED UPON HISTORICAL PAIN."

Instead of finding this healing, Samson found Delilah. She came into his life and slowly chipped away at his character. Her name literally meant "weakness." And she had one: money. And she also *was* one for Samson. Her goal was to get money from the Philistines at his expense. With this goal in mind, she broke down his walls, and eventually he told her the secret to his success.

Then she said to him, "How can you say, 'I love you,' when you won't confide in me? This is the third time you have made a fool of me and haven't told me the secret of your great strength." With such nagging she prodded him day after day until he was sick to death of it.

So he told her everything. "No razor has ever been used on my head," he said, "because I have been a Nazirite dedicated to God from my mother's womb. If my head were shaved, my strength would leave me, and I would become as weak as any other man." (Judges 16:15–17)

Samson ultimately caved to her manipulation. Once she knew that his hair was the source of his power and strength, she lulled him to sleep. "After putting him to sleep on her lap, she called for someone to shave off the seven braids of his hair, and so began to subdue him. And his strength left him" (v. 19). The Philistines ultimately captured Samson, sleeping in the lap of the enemy.

I find it interesting that when the Philistines took Samson, they didn't just throw him in prison. They "seized him, *gouged out his eyes* and took him down to Gaza. Binding him with bronze shackles" (v. 21, emphasis added). They blinded Samson completely! To me, this offers another accurate picture of the enemy's plan for us. Sin wants to bind you and then blind you. Satan wants nothing more than to take away our vision. If he takes away our eyesight and focus on the future, it will prove difficult for us to walk out the journey God has set before us.

Samson's first wife did him dirty.

She got the riddle out of him.

She told the guys.

He went home angry, and while there, he didn't deal with his pain.

Ultimately, he repeated the same mistake again. This is because what you can't get over you will always stay under.

WHAT YOU CAN'T GET OVER YOU WILL ALWAYS STAY UNDER.

DEBILITATED BY REGRET

I remember the weeks and months following my decision to call off things with my once girlfriend. I knew God had asked me to do it. I knew I had ignored him for far too long, and regret consumed my every thought.

I had let down students, friends, and fellow church leaders. I no longer trusted my own decision-making skills. I remember coming home early from work and going straight to bed. Sleep became my crutch, as it does for many going through depression. I even grabbed a copy of the book *What to Say When You're Talking to Yourself,* because my internal monologue was completely focused on this regret. I couldn't get past it.

Distractions can cause you to stray from God's great plan for you and pain can make you delusional, but regret is an ugly trap that can keep you from walking out your day-to-day destiny and unimaginable future.

Just because you've made a mistake or messed up your life in some way doesn't mean your future is hopeless. I've heard many say, "I never imagined my life ending up here. How did I get to this place? This was not supposed to happen this way." Maybe you know God had something better for you but somehow you find yourself in a world of regret today.

I don't think it's wrong to regret your bad decisions. It's

trendy today to post #noregrets and write captions like, "What I did made me who I am today." That's fine for Instagram, but in reality, most of us carry some regret about things we've said yes to that we shouldn't have.

The important thing is not to let regret debilitate you. Samson had no eyes, he was bound, and his enemy would bring him out as entertainment. "While they were in high spirits, they shouted, 'Bring out Samson to entertain us.' So they called Samson out of the prison, and he performed for them" (v. 25).

They would make him play before them and laugh at his expense. "Remember that guy who used to be great! Now he's just a shell of his old person. Bring out Samson so he can entertain us!" they said.

But regret doesn't need to debilitate you. As long as you have a pulse, you still have a chance to accomplish God's plan for your life. There's nothing you can do that can separate you from his love. That's why there's no point in wallowing in regret and letting it prevent you from moving forward.

Though it took Samson being blinded and humiliated to realize this, in the end he knew he still had a chance to fulfill the calling on his life. He knew that God was the God of second chances.

DETERMINED FOR REDEMPTION

Samson prayed as he was bound, beaten, blinded, and broken, "Sovereign LORD, remember me. Please, God, strengthen me just once more, and let me with one blow get revenge on the

Philistines for my two eyes" (Judges 16:28). The story continues with an epic finale:

> Then Samson reached toward the two central pillars on which the temple stood. Bracing himself against them, his right hand on the one and his left hand on the other, Samson said, "Let me die with the Philistines!" Then he pushed with all his might, and down came the temple on the rulers and all the people in it. Thus he killed many more when he died than while he lived. (vv. 29–30)

God knew that Samson, despite his distraction, his pain, and his regret, still had greatness in him. He knew that the promise he had spoken to Samson's parents before he was ever born was still true after all Samson had done wrong. God gave him another shot, and he ultimately fulfilled the plan. He defeated the Philistines and went out with a bang.

If it wasn't too late for Samson, who basically wrote the handbook on What Not to Do, it's not too late for you. You may have made a complete mess in the middle of your life. But God is the only one who can take your mess and turn it into your message.

GOD IS THE ONLY ONE WHO CAN TAKE YOUR MESS AND TURN IT INTO YOUR MESSAGE.

Though Samson's end is inspiring and serves as a beautiful depiction of God's commitment to the plan, his story is really a cautionary tale. Yes, he accomplished a huge, final victory in the last moments of his life, but think of all the victories he missed along the way.

Instead of walking in faith every day, Samson took detours and ended up in a terrible predicament.

I don't know about you, but I want to live a lifetime of small victories instead of only experiencing one epic moment with God. I want my story to look a little something like this:

"Chad got up every day and received joy. He felt the comfort, peace, and strength of the Lord, and he walked with Jesus. He was convinced that he was destined for greatness, and he didn't let his weakness or past regrets distract him from this."

I don't know about you, but I don't want a mess in the middle of my story. I want a message. I want God's plan for every day of my journey, because I know it's better than I could ever conjure up. I want to be in the Faith Hall of Fame not for some huge event but for trying to follow Jesus every day.

Let's do a quick recap of Samson's story and see how your story, along with the time-tested wisdom of the Bible, fits into it.

Samson was destined for greatness.

You are destined for greatness through Jesus. Remember the words of 1 Peter 2:9: "You are a chosen people, a royal priesthood, a holy nation, God's special possession."

Write down three things you feel God wants to do through your life. Choose one to start doing today.

Samson was distracted by weakness.

You, too, can be distracted in the middle of your journey.

First Corinthians 10:13 says, "God *is* faithful; he will not let you be tempted beyond what you can bear. But when you are tempted, he will also provide a way out so that you can endure it" (emphasis added).

Have a game plan for your weakness. Starve it rather than devote your life to it. God has given you Jesus, someone Samson didn't have. He gives you the ability to overcome your weaknesses and move into your potential.

Samson was delusional in pain.

If you haven't already, I guarantee you will experience the pain that comes with being a human being on this earth.

Psalm 147:3 says this about God: "He heals the brokenhearted and binds up their wounds."

If you have pain, don't let it thwart your thinking. You have a healer named Jesus who can set you free.

Samson was debilitated by regret.

You may one day experience the regret that comes with failing at your dream.

Isaiah 1:18 says, "Though your sins are like scarlet, they shall be as white as snow; though they are red as crimson, they shall be like wool."

God has no regret about your failures. He's not living in agony because you messed up. Bring your sin to him, and let him wash it white as snow through Jesus. Because he gave us his only Son, your mistakes are forgotten. This means you can move forward into God's plan!

Samson was determined to pursue greatness.

You can be determined to pursue the greatness God has laid out before you.

Philippians 4:13 says, "I can do all things through Christ who strengthens me" (NKJV).

It's never too late. The God of second chances is waiting to finish your story. You must be determined that through Jesus, you can do all things. That's who Samson was missing in the middle of his mess. With him, you can walk in your destiny.

Chapter Twelve

DON'T JUDGE MY JOURNEY

A few years ago, I was in South Africa, preaching in Cape Town and Pretoria. We happened to have a free day on a Saturday, and the people showing me around town had organized a little surprise. To really follow this story, it's important for you to understand that I'm not a huge nature lover. My idea of a good day involves a coffee shop, not a long-distance hike or horseback-riding excursion. So when they told me, "We have an African safari all lined up for you!" with excited eyes, I did not return the excitement.

You mean we're going out in the middle of nowhere? With a bunch of lions and tigers and bears? No, thank you, is what I thought, but what I said was, "Let's do it."

It was all prepared. The tour was lined up. We were booked to head out in the Jeep in only a couple of hours. I had nowhere to turn. I decided against explaining to them that I was more hood than wilderness, and off we went to see what this safari was all about.

We drove up and arrived at a giant field of nothingness. There were acres and acres of land on either side of us, and I swear I could hear the opening song from *The Lion King* playing somewhere.

Naseebenya gaga geecheee . . . (You know you don't know the lyrics to that song, but you sing it anyway.)

We were in the middle of nowhere and were greeted by one guy holding a rifle, standing in front of a Jeep. I wasn't sure how one guy with a rifle was supposed to protect us from Mufasa and a gang of hyenas, but I had come this far. It seemed I would have to embrace my outdoor side, however deep it was buried.

We all hopped into the Jeep, and the guide began our epic journey. He led us to whatever animal we were hoping to see. We asked to see zebras, and he found zebras. We asked for elephants, and there were some elephants. Lions, giraffes, rhinoceros, hippos . . . He could find them all. Because I had no idea what we were doing, I even asked if we would see a dog. All I got was a blank stare.

In the end, the animals were incredible, and the safari was unforgettable. But what fascinated me most by the end of the day was how well our tour guide knew the landscape. It seemed he had memorized every square inch of that land. Even though we were sitting in a Jeep in the open air where all these animals could rush us at any moment, for some reason I felt at peace. I knew that this tour guide had things under control. He knew where he was leading us the entire time.

I believe God works similarly to a safari tour guide. On this journey of highs and lows that we all walk along, he knows exactly where he's taking us. He understands the lay of the land. He's not just there with you for a moment and then gone. He doesn't drive you out to the savannah and leave you there alone. Instead, he's guiding you during the entire ride, bumps and all.

You can have confidence that God has your journey in the palm of his hand, no matter what others might think or say about it along the way. In the end, it's you and God traveling this path together. This means even those delays and moments when you feel you'll never walk in your future, he's there. This is because he's a covenant-making, covenant-keeping, covenant-enabling God. This is *his* journey.

> HE'S A COVENANT-MAKING, COVENANT-KEEPING, COVENANT-ENABLING GOD. THIS IS *HIS* JOURNEY.

OUR SHEPHERD

King David in the Bible journeyed with God for a long time. He knew what it meant to have good times and bad. As he followed God each day in faith, things weren't always perfect or exciting. He didn't experience all butterflies and rainbows simply because he chose to walk in faith. Though his life is one of greatness and he did ultimately see God's best possible tomorrow, he had successes and failures like the rest of us.

He ruled over Israel for forty years, twenty of which were fantastic and twenty that were a struggle. The huge turn of events that caused the split between these years can be found in 2 Samuel 11. Though David had ruled with God by his side and had seen great success, he still made mistakes and experienced bumps in his journey. "One evening David got up from his bed and walked around on the roof of the palace. From the roof he saw a woman bathing. The woman was beautiful, and David sent someone to find out about her" (vv. 2–3).

You can probably already smell the trouble coming from a mile away. To sum up his giant blunder, David would eventually send for this woman, sleep with her, get her pregnant, and then have her husband killed in war so he could marry her. "The thing David had done displeased the LORD" (v. 27).

Well, duh. Of course it did.

As you can imagine, it's after this point in his journey with God that David began a downward spiral. He walked around with regret and had to face a God he had failed and "displeased."

I think this is one reason why the psalms that David wrote are so beautiful and still carry weight in our lives today. They aren't the prayers and songs of a man who had his act completely together, who achieved all his dreams, who lived every day in God's perfect purpose, or who never encountered hardship on his journey with God. They are the cries of a man who was desperate for God, needing his guidance every step of the way.

As you navigate through the disappointments and depression that come with a broken dream, look to David's psalms for hope.

One of his most famous psalms, and perhaps one of the most famous passages of Scripture, is Psalm 23. In it, David wrote the following words as a seasoned follower of God. He wasn't a new convert, fresh into his journey. Rather, he was nearing the end. He wrote this song after enduring hardships, many that he caused himself. The psalm starts this way:

"The LORD is my shepherd, I lack nothing."

Translation: "Like a tour guide in the savannah with a Jeep and a single shotgun, Jesus is all I need to get through the journey." In this life, it's him plus nothing else. I always like to say,

"If we got Jesus and a cup of coffee, we gonna be all right." (In reality, the cup of coffee is not necessary, but Jesus is!)

David was saying, "God is my leader, the one I'm following." Then he proceeded to paint a beautiful picture of what it means to be a shepherd.

The passage continues:

> He makes me lie down in green pastures,
> he leads me beside quiet waters,
> he refreshes my soul.
> He guides me along the right paths
> for his name's sake. (vv. 2–3)

A shepherd knows where he is leading his sheep just as God knows where he's taking you next. He knows your future steps, because he is the one who initiated the plan before you even met him. He came up with the big idea that is your future, and because of this, he's orchestrating it and unfolding it.

You're not hopping into a car with someone who has no clue where they're going. God knows where the rhinos are and where to find the elephants. He knows where he's leading you on the map, in your spiritual life, in your professional journey, and beyond. He's concerned with every piece of your life and is ready to guide you through it all.

Yes, we could choose to walk away from this plan. We could be a lost sheep or on a safari alone without a guide or a Jeep, pursuing our own misguided idea of success. But if we choose to walk in faith, God will guide us along the way. He'll help us step into the amazing calling he has in store for us.

Let's take a closer look at exactly where this passage says he's leading us:

- Green pastures
- Quiet waters
- Right paths

God's not a demented tour guide. He doesn't drop us off next to the lion pack and tell us to fend for ourselves. He's leading us to happiness and peace. When we journey with God, his goal is not to bring us to places of turmoil, chaos, or distress. He's taking us to a place of tranquility, where we can ultimately find rest inside of our souls.

> **OUR GOD DOESN'T LEAD US INTO FRUSTRATION; HE GUIDES US INTO FULFILLMENT.**

He's also taking us to where the grass is greener. I believe these pastures David is describing are symbols of blessing and provision. David is not referring to a God who's led him to dry land where he can never bear fruit or have success. The journey this shepherd has in store for us is beautiful and life-giving. As you find yourself frustrated with the lows of your journey, remember our God doesn't lead us into frustration; he guides us into fulfillment.

HE KNOWS HOW I'M DOING

Imagine you're on a road trip, and you're sitting in the middle of the back seat. You know, the worst possible seat in the car. The driver in the front is blasting music, all your friends are singing along, and you start to feel queasy. It goes on for a bit, so you decide to speak up.

"Hey, I'm not feeling well. I think we maybe should pull over," you say meekly from the back.

Now imagine that the driver couldn't care less, refusing to turn down the music or inquire what exactly is bothering you. He simply yells back, "Shut up. Enjoy the ride, man! It's all part of the journey!"

I think some of you feel this way about God. You might imagine him as more of a cruel front-seat driver, only focused on getting you to your destination and not concerned about how you're doing every mile of the trip.

I'm happy to report that this is not the way God works. He's full of compassion for you. Jesus said, "The very hairs of your head are all numbered" (Luke 12:7). God cares about every seemingly insignificant detail of our lives. He knows how many hairs are on our heads, what we're thinking about, and how we're feeling on a minute-to-minute basis. The rest of the world only knows how you project your feelings, what you put out on social media or tell your closest friends. But God, he knows how you're really doing.

If he understands the truest form of who you are, then of course he knows when you're not feeling well. And rather than tell you to "suck it up and enjoy the ride," he's ready to comfort you when things get rocky.

David described this quality of God, saying, "He refreshes my soul."

Our souls are who we really are and what's really going on deep inside. They are the central parts of our beings. It's the part that may feel queasy on the road trip of life. David was saying that he needed God to restore who he really was. This included his mind and emotions. And God needs to restore our souls, because sometimes along this journey, our very person begins to crumble. I find this especially true when I've chased after something and failed.

When I feel like a loser and question even my own thinking and worth, my soul is in need of restoration. And it's a restoration only God can give.

We've all gone through the deep soul problems that arise from broken dreams. These are the moments when we feel like giving up on it all and jumping out of the car God is driving. But thankfully he knows when we are feeling this way.

He's like that friend we all have—the one who doesn't just ask, "How are you doing?" This friend waits for you to give a short answer like, "Fine, good, whatever, I'm cool," and then comes in with the big . . .

"But how are you *really* doing?"

These friends, the "really doing" friends, aren't looking for gossip or small talk; they're doing the raw check-in. Their question causes you to expose your true thoughts and bare your soul. God is this type of friend, only he doesn't have to ask. He always knows what's really going on in the back seat of the car and inside our hearts.

Usually when I come home and walk into my house after a long day, I can tell in a split second how my wife is doing. All I do is listen to her tone of voice or watch her body language and I know whether it was a good day or a bad day. I can get an instant read on whether the kids had a nap or didn't, and I know if my girl got to finish her cup of coffee that morning. If she didn't, things aren't pretty.

I may be able to get a read on her status each evening, but only God knows how Julia is really doing. Only God can discern her thoughts, intents, motives, and hurts. I may be able to read a few facial or verbal cues, but God has the only true window into her soul.

You could say that David had gone through some "stuff." Bathsheba ultimately had his baby and that baby died shortly after birth. David knew the sorrow of making mistakes, losing someone he loved, and failing God. But through it all, he had confidence that God knew where he was and would restore his soul despite his failure.

Psalm 23 continues with these famous words: "Even though I walk through the darkest valley, I will fear no evil, for you are with me" (v. 4).

Most of us know what it feels like to have both success and failure on this road of life. The reality is that just because we walk in God's plan doesn't mean we're exempt from dark times. David knew what it meant to have thousands sing his name in the streets. But he also knew what it meant to live with his own failure. And though most of us haven't experienced that kind of adulation, each of us can relate to those moments when things are looking pretty good and those times when life is looking rather bleak. The good news is that we don't have to face these dark valleys alone. We can be free of fear, worry, and doubt!

> **WE CAN CAST OUR CARES UPON GOD BECAUSE WE'RE CONVINCED THAT HE CARES FOR US.**

Why?

Because God is with us and knows exactly what's going on. We can cast our cares upon God because we're convinced that he cares for us.

WHEN TO COMFORT, WHEN TO CORRECT

If he knows what we're going through and he's with us every step of the way, God also must know exactly what we need along this journey. He sees our lows, when life has dealt us a blow, when we face sickness, death, broken relationships, and pain at others' hands. He sees our mistakes, when we mess things up for ourselves, face regret, and hurt those around us. Because of this, God is ready to be both our comforter and our corrector.

In Psalm 23, David walks us through how his life is about God plus nothing else, how God is his shepherd, and how he doesn't care how bleak life may become for him. He knows that even though he cheated on his wife, is hard-pressed on every side, and is going through hell on earth, God will be there for him.

And then he continues with this line: "Your rod and your staff, they comfort me" (v. 4).

The "rod" and "staff" David is referring to point back to the image of a shepherd he's been painting throughout the song. Shepherds in David's day would walk around with a large stick. They would use one side of this stick, the staff, to guide the sheep where they needed to go. This side brought the sheep to peace and tranquility, green pastures, and still waters. The other side of the stick, the rod, was used to correct the sheep when they got off course. Though it wasn't easy for the sheep, the rod ultimately protected them from danger and got them back on the right path.

I am grateful that we serve a God who's not walking around with only one side of the stick. I'm glad my God doesn't just hug me all day, every day. I'm glad he doesn't let me continue to hurt those around me or prevent me from ever learning from my mistakes. I'm glad he brings his rod to smack me over the head sometimes and say, "Get your act together, Chad! That's not how we treat people!"

I'm also thankful that he doesn't walk around beating me up for my failures all day long. I'm glad he doesn't only bring a rod of correction, telling me to shape up and punishing me without bringing comfort and peace.

Our God knows where we are in this journey and when we need to be held and when we need a little discipline. It reminds me of my son Winston. When he wakes up from a nap, he needs about forty-five minutes before he can become a Christian again. During this time, he doesn't want to talk to anyone or do anything. He glares into space and refuses to answer any questions. The only interaction he will allow is for me or his mom to hold him. Julia and I cherish these moments when he only wants to be comforted, because we know in forty-five minutes, we won't be able to get him to sit still.

Then there are other moments when we know a hug is not what Winston needs. When he pushes his baby brother to the ground and leaves him screaming, for instance, Winston does not need a big hug. He needs correction.

Many people find it hard to marry these two facets of God in their minds. *Wait, is he going to love on me or is he going to correct me?* The reality is that it's not one or the other. It's all motivated out of love. It's because he loves you that he carries his rod. Hebrews 12:5–6 describes this quality of God, saying,

"My son, do not make light of the Lord's discipline, and do not lose heart when he rebukes you, because the Lord disciplines the one he loves, and he chastens everyone he accepts as his son."

The devil, on the other hand, does not operate out of love. All he wants to do is fill your life with shame. His desire is to condemn you throughout your day, whispering these types of statements into your ear:

"You're so bad."

"Look what you did now!"

"You'll never amount to anything because of your failure."

"You're from nowhere."

"You're a nobody."

"You'll never walk in your destiny."

If thoughts like these torment you day in and day out, know that these words do not come from God. It's not God telling you that you'll never amount to anything. Even when David cheated and murdered because of lust, God still forgave him. But he also corrected him and got him back on the road to his destiny, which was not an easy one for him to walk.

> **GOD KNOWS WHEN I NEED COMFORT AND WHEN I NEED CORRECTION, AND HE'S COMMITTED TO DOING BOTH.**

David's story proves that God doesn't give up on us, because a true shepherd doesn't lose heart in his sheep and abandon them. Even if the sheep trip up on the journey, the shepherd is ready to comfort and correct when the time is right. I always remind myself that God knows when I need comfort and when I need correction, and he's committed to doing both.

A SEAT AT THE TABLE

Psalm 23 is David's description of his journey with God and his unconditional love. The passage reveals that walking in God's plan is not merely an event or one moment of time. It's a long trek with many ups and downs. There are moments for correction and moments for comfort. There is a valley of death, yet there is no fear. There's a shepherd present every step of the way, guiding you to prosperity, happiness, and peace.

None of us can judge the journey any one person is on, because it's all part of God's plan. I, like you, am a work in progress. I'm not perfect yet, but I'm excited to discover all that God has laid out before me.

I love the way Psalm 23 ends:

> You prepare a table before me
>   in the presence of my enemies.
> You anoint my head with oil;
>   my cup overflows.
> Surely your goodness and love will follow me
>   all the days of my life,
> and I will dwell in the house of the LORD
>   forever. (vv. 5–6)

Just as David prepared a table for Mephibosheth, God has prepared a table for each of us. He wants us to sit at the seat of honor. He wants to overflow our lives with his goodness! I don't know about you, but this sounds like a plan worth pursuing.

It's time to embrace the journey, with its highs and lows, and walk into this plan. It's time to realize that long before you believed in God, you belonged to God. You belonged in his plan. You, even in your brokenness, in your heartbreak, with your patterns of destructive thinking, with your shattered dreams and your messed-up concept of success, have a table prepared for you by God. Once you start chasing after that table and walk with the shepherd who guides, comforts, and brings peace, you'll realize his journey is always better than yours.

> **LONG BEFORE YOU BELIEVED IN GOD, YOU BELONGED TO GOD.**

5 TAKEAWAYS

It's easy to assume that God's plan is one single, amazing event where it will all come together for you. You will achieve something great. You will finish a goal. You will meet the person of your dreams. You will see a city transformed in one single day.

It's a lovely thought, but that's not how God works. God's plan isn't taking us to one moment. His future isn't about a single occurrence. His destiny isn't quite that limited or simple. Walking in faith is a journey. When you say yes to God's plan, you begin experiencing this journey. As we've established, it isn't always easy. And no, you won't always make the right decisions along the way.

Living out God's plan comes with both good times and bad, seasons of success and seasons of failure. Sometimes there's a mess in the middle that is hard to grapple with. Sometimes you go on detours. But no matter what, God is committed to his plan for you.

For some of you, a journey sounds like an exciting adventure. For others, the thought of not knowing and trudging through this plan is daunting. I believe these five takeaways will guide you through the road trip that is walking out God's plan:

1. Say it with me: "I have a destiny."

Say it a few times if you need to. The same way Samson and David had a bright future, you have greatness ahead of you. God's plans for you are big! Don't run from them or feel intimidated by them. Rather, embrace them.

2. Have some resolve.

Notice the determination in Samson's life. Even when he was blinded, beaten, and shackled to two pillars, it wasn't too late for him. This means that it's never too late for you. What have you gotten wrong in your past that you're determined to get right? Write it down, and go after it. It's those who are the most determined to do God's will who see it come to pass.

3. Have faith for the boring seasons.

If you're reading this book and getting amped about all the crazy, epic things that are in store for you on this adventure with God, this takeaway probably depresses you. But the reality is that some of life's moments are dramatic and epic, and some . . . not so much. Maybe you're in the middle of a not-so-glamorous or exciting season. Hold on to faith and trust in the middle of it.

4. Be open to correction.

This one can be difficult to follow. No one's walking around, wanting people to criticize them. But an honest mentor or friend who tells you like it is, points out areas you need to change, and pushes you to be better is invaluable.

"As iron sharpens iron, so one person sharpens another" (Proverbs 27:17). Write down a list of everyone who's sharpening you on your journey. If you have trouble coming up with more than one, then you may need to start developing meaningful relationships with more people who speak truth into your life.

5. Surround yourself with the right people.

Life is like a bus, and on this bus, where you're going is not what matters most. What matters most is who's there with you. Who's on your bus? As you journey through highs and lows, who's traveling along over the bumps with you?

We've already mentioned the need to have friends who speak correction, but you also need to surround yourself with people who inspire you to chase after God's plan, people who stick up for you in your hour of need, and people who challenge you to know God more.

As Ecclesiastes 4:9–10 says,

Two are better than one,
    because they have a good return for their labor:
If either of them falls down,
    one can help the other up.
But pity anyone who falls
    and has no one to help them up.

We weren't meant to go at it alone. God's plan involves us helping each other. On this journey, people matter. Be sure to choose the right ones.

Part Five

THE REASON

What's this plan all about?

Chapter Thirteen

ALWAYS ONLY JESUS

Have you ever had plans fall through? You scheme to have a fun hangout with friends or an amazing party, only for something out of your control to prevent it from happening in the end. Coping with crushed expectations is not the best feeling.

One year on Julia's birthday we had big plans that didn't work out. We were going to fly from Seattle to New York. She had picked out all the restaurants where we would be eating, the stores where we would shop, and the hotel where we would stay. My girl knows how to make a plan. She also knows how to build up hopes, dreams, and wishes for that plan. When a trip or a party is just around the corner, it consumes her every thought. Leading up to our New York trip, it was all she could talk about.

Me: "How was your day, babe?"
Julia: "Five more days until New York!"
Me: "What's for dinner?"
Julia: "Oh man, just wait until we're eating in New
    York. Three more days!"

She was like a kid with a paper-link calendar, counting down the days until Christmas. She was so excited.

And then a little storm hit the East Coast. You've probably heard of it. It wasn't some small rainstorm. It was called Hurricane Sandy. You know once a storm is given a name, it's serious. Let's just say my wife was not a big fan of Sandy. Our bags were packed and we were ready to get on the plane when we turned on the news and learned about this storm. I remember so clearly the confident denial that filled Julia in that very moment.

"It's still fine."

"We can go."

"It'll be fine."

"It's fine."

"It's FINE, okay?!"

I was both afraid *for* her and afraid *of* her. I knew she would have to face the reality of the situation. I knew that our little trip wasn't happening, but I didn't want to be the one to pull the plug on her dreams. I took a seat next to her as she stared at the footage of flooded New York City streets and people blowing to and fro in violent winds. I patted her back. "Sure, sweetie. Yeah, we could still do this."

And then I saw the tears start to well up. In the end, she made the judgment call. We wouldn't be going to NYC that year and drowning in a flood. The trip was off. Happy birthday to her.

Over the course of this book, we've been exploring the plan God has for you and how it's often better than the dreams you've schemed up on your own. His plans are to "prosper you and not to harm you, plans to give you hope and a future" (Jeremiah 29:11). We've explored how Peter, Paul, Jonah, Samson, and others walked in this prosperity and greatness, despite their list of disqualifications, failures, and bumps in the road. We've examined how your plan is unique to your gifts and the people God wants you to impact.

But now it's time to talk about the reason for this plan. I call this the Master Plan. It's the greater plan beneath all other plans, the plan that is greater than man, one that man can barely even imagine. It's the plan that will never fall through like our earthly plans do. It's not a New York City birthday trip that can be canceled due to a storm.

What we're talking about is God's plan for humanity. Each of our lives is merely a piece in the puzzle. As we discover our unique calling, we'll learn more and more that the plan is much bigger than us. This plan's name is Jesus. From the beginning of time, God had a plan to use Jesus, his Son, to save us all. To truly understand this plan, we have to understand his story.

As I've mentioned, I used to think the ultimate plan for my life was something I could achieve with my own strength. I thought my key to success, to walking in accordance with God's plan, was following my Bible-reading schedule and focusing on my actions. If I could just do steps A, B, and C, I'd grow closer to Jesus and, thus, closer to the purpose he'd dreamed up for my life.

IT'S ALL ABOUT JESUS. ALWAYS. ONLY. JESUS.

This may seem odd for someone who professes the gospel of grace to believe, but deep down, I think I always imagined the gospel as a bait and switch. God would bait you with the message of his Son, who died for you, who forgave your sin and extended unconditional grace. Then once you signed your name on the dotted line, things would shift. You would have to get your act together and perform exactly as God wanted you to perform, or else.

But in reality there's no bait and switch. It's all about Jesus. Always. Only. Jesus.

FROM THE VERY BEGINNING

To truly understand God's plan for our lives, we need to go to the start of the story. In Genesis, the first book of the Bible, we learn about creation. God made the day and the night, the plants and the water, and the animals that roam the earth.

> Then God said, "Let us make mankind in our image, in our likeness, so that they may rule over the fish in the sea and the birds in the sky, over the livestock and all the wild animals, and over all the creatures that move along the ground."

> So God created mankind in his own image,
> in the image of God he created them;
> male and female he created them. (Genesis 1:26–27)

Everything was perfect. Because this all went down before sin, the man and woman were flawless. (Just imagine CrossFit bodies without all the CrossFit talk.) But sin eventually ruined it all. A serpent entered the garden of Eden and enticed the woman to disobey the one commandment God had given them. This disobedience would ultimately lead to separation between man and God, years of pain, struggle, and completely unattainable CrossFit bodies. I blame Adam and Eve for not having my own CrossFit body to brag about. Thanks a lot for these tiny calves, guys.

It was after this first sin, all the way back at the very beginning of the story, that God revealed his master plan. He looked to the serpent who had sparked it all, the embodiment of evil, and said, "And I will put enmity between you and the woman, and between your offspring and hers; he will crush your head, and you will strike his heel" (Genesis 3:15).

The "he" in this passage that God is talking about is Jesus! Jesus would ultimately crush Satan underneath his feet by paying the price for sin once and for all and extending grace to all of us. This is the first glimpse in the Bible of God's ultimate goal to end sin and this separation between us and him. This is the first glimpse of his plan, which is Jesus.

PLANNING

There are two types of people in this world—Planners and Anti-Planners. Some people take planning to the next level. Super Duper Planner People are everywhere, and if I'm going to be honest, they scare me. My wife is one of them.

Remember the trip to Hawaii? Well . . . my father-in-law paid for that trip for his four daughters and their families. He paid for the flights, the hotels, the rental cars, and even the food. You ever go to Costco when someone else is paying? I was like Oprah in those aisles of the Hawaii Costco. "You get a Perrier! You get a Perrier!" I was throwing trail mix for four hundred people into the basket.

It was an amazing trip, but what was truly amazing was all the planning that went into it. Julia and her sisters worked on it for almost an entire year. With their dad's credit card, they booked the resort where we would stay, planned our daily activities, and made restaurant reservations. My wife spent most of her days leading up to the trip buying floaties, new swim trunks, and sunscreen. When it came time for Hawaii, we would be ready because of all her master planning. I'm glad I wasn't in charge of the trip. If it had been up to me, we'd just show up and wander the island, confused.

I've always been this way. Growing up, I was never the person who made the five-year plan. Even today I have trouble making a five-day plan. For instance, if someone says to me on a Monday, "Let's hang out on Friday," I immediately start to panic. *What if something comes up that I have to do? What if I'm just not feeling it?* I think.

You might call this having commitment issues, and you might be right.

You're definitely right.

On the other hand, if you ask my wife whether she wants to hang out in January 2021, she'll probably pull out a Google calendar and let you know that Thursday nights would most likely work best for our family.

Planners freak me out. "Oh, one day I'll move here, then I'll get this job over here, maybe I'll grow my hair out at that time, and—"

"Stop!" is what I want to yell at these types of people. "How do you know if that's going to work out?"

Because of this, I'm always super impressed when I see that meticulous planning has gone into something. I remember attending the Hillsong Conference for the first time and being overwhelmed at the level of detail and creativity they put into it. Filled with wonder, I scanned the room full of thirty thousand people. I saw the lighting cues, the screens, the art and creativity.

I asked myself, *How long have they been working on this? A year? Two years?* There must have been a huge team devoted to the conference for at least that long. And I knew they would simply start again, planning for next year, the moment the conference was over.

> **GOD'S RESOLVE FOR RELATIONSHIP IS THE REASON FOR HIS PLAN.**

If I think one year of planning is remarkable, I can barely even wrap my head around how long God has had a plan for us.

At the start of the story of man (we're talking a long, long time ago), he was saying, "I know what I want to do with these people." Further back than we can even fathom, God planned for Jesus to come and defeat evil so that he could have a relationship with us. God's resolve for relationship is the reason for his plan.

ALWAYS BAILING US OUT

Starting with the garden of Eden incident and then continuing after that, something kept getting in the way of God's original plan for relationship. And, funny enough, that something was the reason he had the plan to begin with! It was us.

Instead of obeying the God who created us, we rebelled against his will. And we did it over and over again throughout history. If you look in the Old Testament, you'll see how humans continued to mess things up for themselves. We saw this in Jonah's and Samson's stories, and we can see this in many others. What's remarkable about these stories is that in each case, every time humans fail, God comes to them with love. And often, the ones he extends love to still choose to turn their backs on him.

Let's take a look at the story of the Israelites. The Bible tells how the Egyptians "made their lives bitter with harsh labor in brick and mortar and with all kinds of work in the fields; in all their harsh labor the Egyptians worked them ruthlessly" (Exodus 1:14). In response to this suffering, God found a man named Moses and told him of his plans, saying:

> I have indeed seen the misery of my people in Egypt. I have heard them crying out because of their slave drivers, and I am concerned about their suffering. So I have come down to rescue them from the hand of the Egyptians and to bring them up out of that land into a good and spacious land, a land flowing with milk and honey. (3:7–8)

The Israelites cried out for freedom from slavery, and God ultimately delivered them. You'd think they would've been stoked! He was taking them to something better than they could have ever imagined. He wasn't merely freeing them; he was going to give them milk and honey. Their next move? Worshipping fake gods and whining out in the wilderness! The sin cycle continued for hundreds of years, and each time God would come in and bail them out.

I've met many in my life who follow this cyclical pattern with their struggles. There was a young man at our church whose mom had been working with us because he struggled with a serious addiction. This mom was always so worried about her son and had placed him in rehab countless times. She often called on our church staff to pray for him or meet with him in his hour of need. It was an ugly situation, but what made it even uglier was the fact that her son would repeatedly give up on rehab and return to his addiction.

Every time this happened, his mom would bail him out and bring him back again. No matter how many times he messed up, she drove him back to the safety of rehab.

Why would she do this after he failed her repeatedly? Easy. Because she loved her son, and that love came with commitment.

It's the same with God. He was committed to his master plan of relationship, so he bailed humans out and returned to them over and over again. Before the Jesus portion of this plan came into effect, God made "the law." With the same goal for relationship, the law was a series of regulations that made it so humanity could be in harmony with him. He asked the people to sacrifice animals to him to atone for their wrongdoing. He gave them a series of rules to live by. I challenge you to read about these rules in Leviticus with a new lens. Instead of viewing them as rigid and legalistic, view them as God's aim for relationship. He made the old law because he loved people enough to offer a chance for them to reach up to him from out of their sin.

But something had to change. God had bailed humanity out too many times, and humanity just couldn't seem to keep up with his rules.

The old plan was only a hint of the good things in the new plan. Since that old "law plan" wasn't complete in itself, it couldn't complete those who followed it. No matter how many sacrifices were offered year after year, they never added up to a complete solution. (Hebrews 10:1 THE MESSAGE)

I love the way this passage builds up to the new plan God made for us. He saw that we couldn't do things by our own strength. He saw that we'd often pursue our own dreams or our own image of success and fall flat on our faces. He saw that no matter how many rules we followed, we would never be in true relationship until he restructured a way for our salvation. He had to find a way for us to walk in his dream. God looked at us and said, "I want to be with these people." He wanted to return to the relationship he had with us in the garden of Eden.

Because of this, he said, "I will send a redeemer."

All throughout the Old Testament, Isaiah, Jeremiah, Micah, and the rest of the prophets foretold the coming of this redeemer. God looked at humanity and knew that something in the system was broken. A wall had risen between God and humanity, preventing the relationship that God had so hoped for, and Jesus was the answer.

God sent Jesus so that those who believed in him would have everlasting life and relationship with him. He broke the wall of separation once and for all, and now we no longer need that bailout.

When Jesus, the one who it's all about, the ultimate plan, showed up on the scene, he waited thirty years to perform his first miracle and reveal to the world who he really was. Not too long after this, he went to the synagogue, opened a scroll, and read to everyone there a prophecy about himself.

I don't recommend doing this if you're not Jesus. It's always a little socially awkward when someone reads an article or tweet about themselves in front of others. You know it's never comfortable when someone slyly slips into the conversation, "It's says here, 'I'm a vanguard in my field,'" or "You know my

CrossFit instructor says I'm one of the strongest he's seen," or "Look at this Instagram comment that says how pretty I look in my selfie!"

We don't care. We now think you're narcissistic.

But Jesus got away with it. At the very start of his ministry, he grabbed the scroll and read this scripture from the book of Isaiah:

> The Spirit of the Sovereign LORD is on me,
>> because the LORD has anointed me
>> to proclaim good news to the poor.
> He has sent me to bind up the brokenhearted,
>> to proclaim freedom for the captives
>> and release from darkness for the prisoners,
> to proclaim the year of the LORD's favor. (61:1–2)

The story continues with Jesus mic-dropping like a boss. "Then he rolled up the scroll, gave it back to the attendant and sat down. The eyes of everyone in the synagogue were fastened on him. He began by saying to them, 'Today this scripture is fulfilled in your hearing'" (Luke 4:20–21).

Boom! Jesus was talking about the plan, the fulfillment of God's goal for relationship. The words he read that day had been spoken more than four hundred years before he would ever fulfill them, revealing that God had it all laid out from the start.

Jesus showed up to bring freedom and bail humanity out once and for all. He told his followers:

> I am the Good Shepherd. I know my own sheep and my own
> sheep know me. In the same way, the Father knows me and

I know the Father. I put the sheep before myself, sacrificing myself if necessary. You need to know that I have other sheep in addition to those in this pen. I need to gather and bring them, too. They'll also recognize my voice. Then it will be one flock, one Shepherd. This is why the Father loves me: because I freely lay down my life. And so I am free to take it up again. No one takes it from me. I lay it down of my own free will. I have the right to lay it down; I also have the right to take it up again. I received this authority personally from my Father. (John 10:14–18 THE MESSAGE)

Jesus had a sense of his mission. He knew that God had a plan for his life and that he would be the ultimate hope for humanity. He knew he was called to be the shepherd David talked about, to care for the sheep and lay down his life for people. Jesus knew he was the Master Plan. Just as God has a plan for you, God had a plan for his Son. And Jesus modeled for us how to confidently walk in that plan.

He said, "This is why I'm here. I know what God made me to do. I will gladly lay down my life for you so that God no longer has to bail you out. I will sacrifice my life so that God will remember your sin no more . . . so that you can be healed, saved, free, and have everlasting life."

STICK TO THE PLAN

When I first started making plans to move to LA and start Zoe Church, my friend Aaron was right there with me. He was ready to be a part of the church we would one day build. A couple of years into the planning process, he went on a trip with me to Australia.

While we were there, we received some news that threw a wrench into the whole plan. We were in the hotel room, and he was pacing back and forth, shaking his head, saying, "What are we going to do now? Is the plan still the same?"

I remember being filled with confidence. I knew that what I had heard from God years before in a church service was still the same. The plan for a church that he had dropped on me, that I had written out on my first-generation iPad, still stood.

I looked at him and said, "We're going to stick to the plan."

Throughout all human history, God never wavered from his original plan. In the Old Testament and the New, he was filled with love for his people and desired to be reconciled to them. Despite human failings and missteps throughout this journey, God never got distracted from or gave up on his purpose and mission for us. He didn't look at the whining Israelites in the wilderness and say, "Meh. I think I'll make another plan. I think I'll focus on animals now instead of humans." God didn't have a plan B. He only had a plan A. And plan A was Jesus Christ.

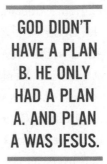

GOD DIDN'T HAVE A PLAN B. HE ONLY HAD A PLAN A. AND PLAN A WAS JESUS.

Now that we've discovered what the plan is really about, how do we stick to it? It's simple. Have faith in the person of Jesus, and realize that your unique calling and God Dream tie back to him. Don't get caught up in legalism or religious practices like I did. Don't walk around thinking it's your accomplishments that give you the ability to live God's future. Don't strive by your own strength to get out of your destructive thinking and disappointment. Make everything about Jesus and your relationship with

God, and watch how easy it is to move past all else into the best possible tomorrow.

If your calling is to start a nonprofit that rescues people from trafficking, then trust that God rescued you through Jesus and offer that same love to the people your organization serves.

If God has gifted you with a platform to speak, don't shrink away. Remember the words of Philippians 4:13, and know that you can do all things "through [Christ] who gives me strength." Christ came to set you free from fear.

If your plan involves being an amazing mother, wife, father, or husband, remember how Christ laid down his life for the church. Understand how God's larger plan involved sacrificing the rights of his only Son, and let that have a powerful ripple effect in the life of your family.

God has a plan for your life, and that specific plan always comes back to Jesus.

Romans 12:9 says, "Cling to what is good." Let's hold fast to the reality of Christ and God's original plan for relationship and never let go. Let's stop allowing the enemy to take us back to a place where we need to be bailed out or a place where we're separated from God. Let's not pretend the old plan of the law is still intact and make our lives about following codes of conduct.

Let's stick to plan A.

Let's stick to Jesus.

5 TAKEAWAYS

I hope you see your future and your tomorrow as a little brighter. My aim is that you would leave this book with a greater understanding of God's purpose for you. He's always had one. He's been at work before you were born to "prosper you," to "give you hope and a future."

He's seen your ups and downs, your highs and lows. He knows your stories and your quirks. He created those quirks, after all. Now he's just waiting for you to take the step of faith. As you start taking steps each day, I'm convinced you'll discover a life full of purpose. Let me leave you with five more takeaways to encourage you as you walk out your best possible tomorrow:

1. Choose God's plan over yours.

    Write down the last five prayers you've made to God. If the prayer included an ask for something you wanted, write "Me" next to it. If it included something God wanted, write "God." Where do your prayers lean?

2. Get involved with people.

    I can't stress enough the importance of living your life

for others. A great place to start is the local church. The church plays a huge role in Christ's plan for the world. Get involved. Better yet, get planted. If you commit yourself to being an active part of the work that is happening in your church, you'll have a front-row seat to God's plan.

3. Stay patient.

You should be excited to walk out this plan. But don't get discouraged by delays. When it doesn't look like things are going as planned, remind yourself that God is working things out behind the scenes.

4. Live the Zoe life.

Jesus came so that you could "have life, and have it to the full." These are the words of John 10:10 in the Bible, and they prove that part of God's plan is for you to enjoy this life on earth. In the Greek, the word John uses in this verse is *Zoe*, and it means taking in and enjoying the abundance and fullness of this life on earth.

Try not to take your life too seriously. No one else does.

Learn to laugh at yourself often. Take breaks from your work. Enjoy your hobbies. Experience this fullness that Jesus was talking about in John. If you're leaving this book ready to walk out the plan, try not to approach it too seriously.

5. Respect the process.

We are all in the process. There are no shortcuts. There are no gimmicks. There is no such thing as a five-step program that gives you everything you ever wanted. This journey with God, your role in his church, it takes time and there's a learning curve.

I get excited when I think about you, reader, and all you can accomplish with Jesus. I get excited knowing you can move past your broken dreams. I get excited for the church of tomorrow that will only get better and better. I get excited knowing that your unique gifts, talents, strengths, and journey will make the church the vibrant, life-giving, hope-filled gift that it was meant to be.

Oh, the possibilities!

ACKNOWLEDGMENTS

my queen: julia
our best friends: georgia, winston, and mav
the greatest people on the planet: the people of ZOE LA
our amazing staff and elders: rich jr, pastor jude, and dave
    patterson
my parents: dave and windy veach
leslie harter: none of this happens without you
mark johnson: creative genius

NOTES

1. Javier G. Polavieja and Lucinda Platt, "Nurse or Mechanic? The Role of Parental Socialization and Children's Personality in the Formation of Sex-Typed Occupational Aspirations," *Social Forces* 93, no. 1 (Sept. 2014): 31–61, https://muse.jhu.edu/article/554382 /pdf; John Haltiwanger, "When I Grow Up . . . Why Only 6 Percent of Us Achieve Our Childhood Dreams," *Elite Daily*, Nov. 19, 2014, http://elitedaily.com/money/entrepreneurship/only-6 -percent-of-people-acheive-their-childhood-dreams/855270/.
2. Carolyn Gregoire, "The 75-Year Study That Found the Secrets to a Fulfilling Life," *Huffington Post*, Aug. 11, 2013, http:// www.huffingtonpost.com/2013/08/11/how-this-harvard -psycholo_n_3727229.html.
3. Oliver Leiber, 1989, BMG Music.
4. Andrew Sergeyev, "20 Leadership Quotes on Focus to Inspire You," Timewiser, http://timewiser.com /blog/20-inspiring-leadership-quotes-on-focus/.

ABOUT THE AUTHOR

Chad Veach is lead pastor of Zoe LA in Los Angeles, California. Zoe LA is a young, thriving church with a goal of infusing Zoe "life" and God's love into people from all backgrounds and walks. Chad is also an internationally known speaker who travels with the message of this life and the hope that is found in Jesus. He is the author of *Unreasonable Hope*, a book that recounts the story of how his family dealt with a heartbreaking diagnosis and provides faith-building insight and biblical truths for those facing struggles of their own.

Twitter: www.twitter.com/chadcveach
Instagram: www.instagram.com/chadcveach
Facebook: www.facebook.com/chadcveach
www.zoechurch.org